The Chartered Institute of Marketing

Chartered Postgraduate Diploma in Marketing-Stage One

STUDY TEXT

Emerging Themes

2010 edition

Second edition August 2010

First edition July 2009

ISBN 9780 7517 8943 0
(Previous ISBN 9780 7517 6816 9)

e ISBN 9780 7517 9151 8

British Library Cataloguing-in-Publication Data
A catalogue record for this book
is available from the British Library

Published by

BPP Learning Media Ltd
Aldine House, Aldine Place
London W12 8AA

www.bpp.com/learningmedia

Printed in the United Kingdom

All our rights reserved. No part of this publication may be reproduced, stored in a retrieval system or transmitted, in any form or by any means, electronic, mechanical, photocopying, recording or otherwise, without the prior written permission of BPP Learning Media Ltd.

We are grateful to the Chartered Institute of Marketing for permission to reproduce in this text the syllabus, tutor's guidance notes and past examination questions.

Author: Angela Hatton
Thanks to Kate Machattie for her input to this second edition.
Template design: Yolanda Moore
Photography: Terence O'Loughlin

Your learning materials, published by BPP Learning Media Ltd, are printed on paper sourced from sustainable, managed forests.

©
BPP Learning Media Ltd
2010

A note about copyright

Dear Customer

What does the little © mean and why does it matter?

Your market-leading BPP books, course materials and e-learning materials do not write and update themselves. People write them: on their own behalf or as employees of an organisation that invests in this activity. Copyright law protects their livelihoods. It does so by creating rights over the use of the content.

Breach of copyright is a form of theft – as well as being a criminal offence in some jurisdictions, it is potentially a serious breach of professional ethics.

With current technology, things might seem a bit hazy but, basically, without the express permission of BPP Learning Media:

- Photocopying our materials is a breach of copyright
- Scanning, ripcasting or conversion of our digital materials into different file formats, uploading them to facebook or emailing them to your friends is a breach of copyright

You can, of course, sell your books, in the form in which you have bought them – once you have finished with them. (Is this fair to your fellow students? We update for a reason.) But the e-products are sold on a single user licence basis: we do not supply 'unlock' codes to people who have bought them second-hand.

And what about outside the UK? BPP Learning Media strives to make our materials available at prices students can afford by local printing arrangements, pricing policies and partnerships which are clearly listed on our website. A tiny minority ignore this and indulge in criminal activity by illegally photocopying our material or supporting organisations that do. If they act illegally and unethically in one area, can you really trust them?

Contents

Introduction

• Aim of the Study Text • Studying for CIM qualifications • The Chartered Postgraduate Syllabus • CIM's Magic Formula • Assessment format • A guide to the features of the Study Text • A note on Pronouns • Additional resources • Your personal study plan v

Chapters

1 Emerging themes in context 1
2 Environmental information 19
3 Evaluating and assessing emerging themes 37
4 Emerging themes in organisations' environment 53
5 Emerging themes within organisations 79

Key concepts   101

Index   103

Review form & free prize draw

1 Aim of the Study Text

This book has been deliberately referred to as a 'Study Text' rather than text book, because it is designed to help you through your specific CIM Chartered Postgraduate Diploma in Marketing studies. It covers Unit 1 Emerging Themes.

So, why is it similar to, but not actually, a text book? Well, CIM has identified key texts that you should become familiar with. The purpose of this Study Text is not to replace these texts but to pick out the important parts that you will definitely need to know in order to pass, simplify these elements and, to suggest a few areas within the texts that will provide good additional reading but that are not absolutely essential. We will also suggest a few other sources and useful press and CIM publications which are worth reading.

We know some of you will prefer to read text books from cover to cover, whilst others amongst you will prefer to pick out relevant parts or dip in and out of the various topics. This Study Text will help you to ensure that if you are a 'cover to cover' type, then you will not miss the emphasis of the syllabus. If you are a 'dip in and out' type, then we will make sure that you find *the* parts which are essential for you to know. Unlike a standard text book which will have been written to be used across a range of alternative qualifications, this Study Text has been specifically written for your CIM course.

Throughout this Study Text you will find real examples of marketing in practice as well as key concepts highlighted.

2 Studying for CIM qualifications

There are a few key points to remember as you study for your CIM qualification:

(a) You are studying for a **professional** qualification. This means that you are required to use professional language and adopt a business approach in your work.

(b) You are expected to show that you have 'read widely'. Make sure that you read the quality press (and don't skip the business pages), read Marketing, The Marketer, Research and Marketing Week avidly.

(c) Become aware of the marketing initiatives you come across on a daily basis. For example, when you go shopping look around and think about why the store layout is as it is: consider the messages, channel choice and timings of ads when you are watching TV. It is surprising how much you will learn just by taking an interest in the marketing world around you.

(d) Get to know the way CIM writes its exam papers and assignments. CIM uses a specific approach(the Magic Formula) to ensure a consistent approach when designing assessment materials. Make sure you are fully aware of this, as it will help you interpret what the examiner is looking for (a full description of the Magic Formula appears later and is heavily featured within the chapters).

(e) Learn how to use Harvard referencing. This is explained in detail in our CIM Chartered Professional Diploma- Stage One Assessment Workbook.

(f) Ensure that you read very carefully all assessment details sent to you by CIM. CIM is very strict with regard to deadlines and completing the correct paperwork to accompany any assignment or project. Failing to meet any assessment entry deadlines or completing written work on time will mean that you will have to wait for the next round of assessment dates and will need to pay the relevant assessment fees again.

3 The Chartered Postgraduate Syllabus

The Chartered Postgraduate Diploma in Marketing is aimed at Brand Managers, Strategic Marketing Managers, Business Development Managers and middle to senior Marketing Managers. If you are a graduate, you will be expected to have covered a minimum of half your credits in marketing subjects. You are therefore expected at this level of the qualification to demonstrate the ability to manage marketing resources and contribute to business decisions from a marketing perspective or senior marketing management and pass the Entry test to level 7.

The aim of the qualification is to provide the knowledge and skills for you to develop an 'ability to do' in relation to marketing planning. CIM qualifications concentrate on applied marketing within real work-places.

The complete Chartered Postgraduate qualification is split into two stages. Stage 1 comprises 4 units. Stage 2 is a work based project to enable students to gain Chartered Marketer status immediately.

The Stage 1 qualification is made from four units:

- Unit 1 Emerging Themes
- Unit 2 Analysis and Decision
- Unit 3 Marketing Leadership and Planning
- Unit 4 Managing Corporate Reputation

The syllabus, as provided by CIM, can be found below with reference to our coverage within this study text.

Unit characteristics

Students should be able to critically evaluate the impact of a range of new and emerging themes on marketing, business organisations and the changing marketing environment. In addition, this unit will also help students to build and refine the skills necessary to anticipate and adapt to future changes. In undertaking a critical evaluation of the key themes, students should be able to take a strategic perspective of the impact of these themes at a sectoral or industry level, as well as upon the organisation they work for, or another one they know well.

By the end of the unit, students should be able to critically assess and evaluate the significance of various emerging themes, to demonstrate an ability to recognise the strategic importance of key themes, and to consider how best to take them into account when developing and implementing marketing strategies. Finally, by the end of the unit, students will have established strategies and mechanisms for anticipating future trends and emerging themes.

Note the syllabus includes the themes, but the actual content (examples below in brackets) will be updated annually to reflect the one, two or three most influential recent developments.

Potential macro-environmental emerging themes:

- Political (eg devolution, network governance)
- Economic (eg credit crunch)
- Social (eg changing demographics, migration, health and obesity)
- Technological (eg emerging technologies and their impact on business, social networking, 3D printing)
- Environmental (eg climate change)

Potential meso-environmental emerging themes:

- Marketing's new ground (eg societal/social and green marketing, digital marketing)
- Changing consumers (eg customer power, ethical consumption)
- Changing nature of competition and supply chains (eg collaboration and competition)

Potential micro-environmental themes:

- Contemporary business strategies (eg business sustainability and the triple bottom line)
- The marketing professional (eg intelligence gathering, creative and flexible thinking)

Overarching learning outcomes

By the end of this unit students should be able to:

- Critically evaluate a range of key emerging macro-environmental themes and make a critical assessment of their significance for a specific sector or industry
- Propose strategic marketing responses to the key emerging themes judged to have the greatest potential impact on a specific sector. Responses should reflect contemporary marketing practice (ie marketing's new ground) and demonstrate creativity.

SECTION 1 – Macro and meso emerging themes (weighting 50%)

		Covered in chapter(s)
1.1	Critically evaluate macro-environmental emerging themes and assess/forecast their potential impact upon one specific sector or industry: • Changes in political governance systems and political focus • Contemporary economic opportunities/challenges • Social change (at local and global levels) • Emerging technologies • Environmental challenges • Methods of forecasting/predicting change	1, 2, 3 & 4
1.2	Critically evaluate meso-environmental themes and assess/forecast their potential impact upon a specific sector or industry: • Changes in consumer behaviour • Changes in nature/structure of competition • Changes in nature/structure of supply chains	1, 2, 3 & 4

SECTION 2 – Meso and micro emerging themes (weighting 50%)

		Covered in chapter(s)
2.1	Judge the importance of a range of emerging themes to a particular organisation: • Scenario planning • Impact/risk assessment	5
2.2	Develop contemporary strategic marketing and business responses to a prioritised emerging theme: • Marketing's 'new ground' • Contemporary business strategies	5
2.3	Propose methods by which marketing professionals can anticipate and adapt to change: • Sources of data and intelligence • Developing intellectual skills and creativity • New forms of networking	5

4 CIM's Magic Formula

The Magic Formula is a tool used by CIM to help both examiners write exams and assignment tasks and you to interpret what you are being asked to write about. It is useful for helping you to check that you are using an appropriate balance between theory and practice for each unit.

Contrary to the title, there is nothing mystical about the Magic Formula and simply knowing it (or even mentioning it in an assessment) will not automatically secure a pass. What it does do however is to help you to check that you are presenting your answers in an appropriate format, including enough marketing theory, and applying it to a real marketing context or issue. Students working through the range of CIM qualifications are expected to evaluate to a greater extent, and apply a more demanding range of marketing decisions, as they progress from the lower to the higher levels. At the Chartered Postgraduate Diploma level, there will be an emphasis on evaluation.

Graphically, the Magic Formula for the Chartered Postgraduate Diploma in Marketing is shown below:

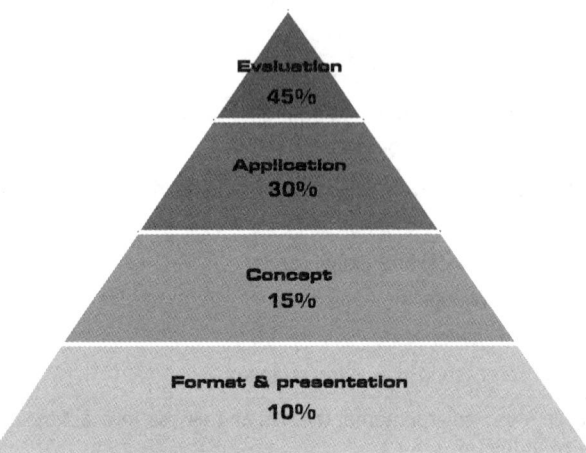

The Magic Formula for the Chartered Postgraduate Diploma in Marketing

You can see from the pyramid that for the Chartered Postgraduate Diploma marks are awarded in the following proportions:

- **Presentation and format – 10%**

    Remember you are expected to present your work professionally which means that it should ALWAYS be typed and attention should be paid to making it look as visually appealing as possible. It also means that CIM will stipulate the format in which you should present your work. The assessment formats you will be given will be varied and can include things like reports, slides, emails, memos, formal letters, press releases, discussion documents, briefing papers, agendas, and newsletters.

- **Concept – 15%**

    Concept refers to your ability to state, recall and describe marketing theory. The definition of marketing is a core CIM syllabus topic. If we take this as an example, you would be expected to recognise, recall, and write this definition to a word perfect standard to gain the full marks for concept. Understanding marketing concepts is clearly the main area where marks will be given within your assessment.

- **Application – 30%**

    Application based marks are given for your ability to apply marketing theories to real life marketing situations. For example, you may be asked to discuss the definition of marketing, and how it is applied within your own organisation. Within this sort of question 30% of the marks would have been awarded within the 'concept' aspect of the Magic Formula. You will gain the rest of the marks through your ability to evaluate to what extent the concept is applied within your own organisation. Here you are not only using the definition but are applying it in order to consider the market orientation of the company.

- **Evaluation – 45%**

    Evaluation is the ability to assess the value or worth of something, sometimes through careful consideration of related advantages and disadvantages or weighing up of alternatives. Results from your evaluation should enable you to discuss the importance of an issue, using evidence to support your opinions.

    Using the example of you being asked whether or not your organisation adopts a marketing approach. If you were asked to 'evaluate' this, you should provide reasons and specific examples of why you think it might take this approach, as well as considering why it might not take this approach, before coming to a final conclusion.

5 Assessment format

The assessment for *Emerging Themes* will require you to prepare a discussion paper covering themes arising from CIM's list of emerging, contemporary issues. This list will be annually updated.

6 A guide to the features of the Study Text

Each of the chapter features (see below) will help you to break down the content into manageable chunks and ensure that you are developing the skills required for a professional qualification.

Chapter feature	Relevance and how you should use it	Corresponding icon
Chapter topic list	Study the list, each numbered topic denotes a numbered section in the chapter	–
Introduction	Shows why topics need to be studied and is a route guide through the chapter	–
Syllabus linked Learning Objectives	Outlines what you should learn within the chapter based on what is required within the syllabus	–
Format & Presentation	Outlines a key marketing presentation format with reference to the Magic Formula	(10%)
Concept	A key concept to learn with reference to the Magic Formula	(15%)
Application	An example of applied marketing with reference to the Magic Formula	(30%)
Evaluation	An example of evaluation with reference to the Magic Formula	(45%)
Activity	An application-based activity for you to complete	✏
Key text links	Emphasises key parts to read in a range of other texts and other learning resources	📚
Marketing at work	A short case study to illustrate marketing practice	📰
Assignment tip	Key advice based on the assignment	✓
Quick quiz	Use this to check your learning	
Objective check	Use this review what you have learnt	

7 A note on Pronouns

On occasions in this Study Text, 'he' is used for 'he or she', 'him' for 'him or her' and so forth. Whilst we try to avoid this practice it is sometimes necessary for reasons of style. No prejudice or stereotyping according to sex is intended or assumed.

8 Additional resources

8.1 CIM's supplementary reading list

We have already mentioned that CIM requires you to demonstrate your ability to 'read widely'. CIM issues an extensive reading list for each unit. For this unit CIM recommends supplementary reading. Within the Study Text we have highlighted within the wider reading links specific topics where these resources will help. CIM's supplementary reading list for this unit is:

Parsons, E. and Maclaran, P. (2009) Contemporary issues in marketing and consumer behaviour, Butterworth Heinemann, Oxford.

Toffler, A. and Toffler, H. (2006) Revolutionary wealth. Knopf, London.

Tapscott, D. and Williams, A.D. (2008) Wikinomics: how mass collaboration changes everything. Atlantic books.

Porter, M.E. (2004) Competitive strategy: techniques for analyzing industries and competitors. NY, Free Press, New York.

8.2 Assessment preparation materials from BPP Learning Media

To help you pass the entire Stage 1 of the Chartered Postgraduate Diploma in Marketing we have created a complete study package. **The Chartered Postgraduate Diploma Assessment Workbook** covers all four units for the Postgraduate Diploma level. Practice question and answers, tips on tackling assignments and work-based projects are included to help you succeed in your assessments.

Our A6 set of spiral bound **Passcards** are handy revision cards that are ideal to reinforce key topics for the Chartered Postgraduate Diploma in Marketing.

9 Your personal study plan

Preparing a Study Plan (and sticking to it) is one of the key elements to learning success.

Think about the number of hours you should dedicate to your studies. Guided learning hours will include time spent in lesson, working on fully prepared distance learning materials, formal workshops and work set by your tutor. We also know that to be successful, students should spend *at least* the same amount of time spent working through guided learning conducting self study. This means that for the entire qualification with four units you should spend time working in a tutor guided manner and at least the same time completing recommended reading, working on assignments, and revising for exams. This Study Text will help you to organise this portion of self study time.

Now think about the exact amount of time you have (don't forget you will still need some leisure time!) and complete the following tables to help you keep to a schedule.

	Date	Duration in weeks
Course start		
Course finish		Total weeks of course:

Assignment submission date	Assignment prep to commence	Total weeks to complete the final assignment:

Content chapter coverage plan

Chapter	To be completed by	Incorporated into assignment
1 Emerging themes in context		
2 Environmental information		
3 Evaluating and assessing emerging themes		
4 Emerging themes in organisations' environment		
5 Emerging themes within organisations		

Chapter 1
Emerging themes in context

Topic list

1 PEST and STEEPLE revisited
2 Change and the planning gap
3 The Business Reality
4 An emerging theme

Introduction

This chapter will enable you to review what you've learnt in earlier CIM studies about the nature and importance of the external environment.

A strategic approach to marketing is built on the organisation being outward looking rather than just internally focussed. That external view of the world starts with clarity about the sector it operates in and how it is changing. Macro level forces drive the fortunes of sectors and organisations – they are the catalysts for strategic wear-out for businesses which fail to identify and respond robustly to changes. These changes impact on the market environment in which organisations operate. The credit crunch encourages consumers to be more conservative in their spending and new technology may introduce new types of competitor or customer solutions.

It is the changing environment and emerging themes which make the task of marketing both challenging and dynamic. A solution that had competitive advantage yesterday may have a short life span if the customer's needs and priorities change.

The syllabus for this Unit is not topic specific; it will evolve in real time to reflect the emerging themes in your sector and industry. You should find it highly relevant to your current role. It will also help you build the attitude and skills needed to be aware of future emerging themes.

 ACTIVITY 1 application

Throughout this module you will be directed to different sources of information for research and further reading. Take time as you do this to do two things:

1. Check the source in terms of its relevance to your sector – keep a list of useful sources and websites. It will save you time later.
2. Think about the articles you are reading– pay attention to style and tone.

Syllabus linked learning objectives

By the end of the chapter you will be able to:

	Learning objectives	Syllabus link
1	Justify the need to monitor the macro environment and make changes to strategy as a result	1.1, 1.2
2	Critically assess the broad macro environmental factors and how they impact differently on different sectors and organisations - leading potentially to strategic wear-out	1.1, 1.2
3	Understand how this environment changes and the nature of 'emerging themes'	1.1, 1.2
4	Be able to explain how environmental changes impact on different sectors and the performance of organisations	1.1, 1.2
5	Appreciate the resulting changes for strategic marketing and the work of professional marketers	1.1, 1.2
6	Have identified how recent environmental changes have impacted on a specific sector	Entire syllabus

1 PEST and STEEPLE revisited

Business does not operate within a vacuum. A solid understanding of the external environment (as you should already know) is vital for the marketer.

1.1 PEST and STEEPLE

Industry and sectors operate in a dynamic and ever changing external environment. This external environment consists of a number of forces that cannot be directly changed by the organisations (individually or collectively) within the sector, but which impact directly and indirectly on the sector and the organisations within it.

You are likely to be familiar with these from earlier CIM studies. Often referred to by the mnemonics PEST or STEEPLE these forces are outlined in the following table.

PEST	STEEPLE
Political and Legal	**S**ocial, cultural and demographic
Economic	**T**echnological
Social, cultural and demographic	**E**conomic and demographic
Technological and environmental	**E**nvironmental
	Political
	Legal
	Ethical

This external environment drives the fortunes of the sectors and organisation, generating both opportunities that can be exploited (or missed) and threats that can be anticipated (or addressed head on).

This has always been the same – external environments change. The technological development of the internal combustion engine replaced the pony and cart; candle makers lost sales when gas lamps and later electricity were made available to homes. The difference today is the speed of change. In the past environments changed slowly, new technology took years to be commercialised, social and cultural changes were all more predictable in a population that was less connected and mobile. When change is slow organisations have plenty of time to react to it – forecasting is less of a requirement.

Today the external environment changes rapidly, sometimes unexpectedly. The credit crunch demonstrates only too clearly how swift and significant change can be. An interconnected global economy suffered the aftershocks of the sub-prime problems in the USA almost simultaneously.

Look at the impact the credit crunch had on Ireland, once dubbed the Celtic Tiger because of its high economic growth rates:

"The Irish economy shrank by 7.5% in the last three months of 2008 compared with the same period a year earlier. The construction industry, which had been a catalyst of Irish growth in earlier years, suffered a 24% fall in output, the biggest fall on record. In the whole of 2008 the economy shrank by 2.3%, the first decline since 1983."

Source: Central Statistics Office (CSO, 2009)

You can see just from this small example that an environmental change can impact on performance at country as well as company level, but that change may not be felt equally by all sectors or firms within a sector. The focus of this Unit is at sector or industry level rather than organisation level. However we shall look at both to demonstrate the importance of awareness and vigilance in market analysis. For example:

- As a result of the credit crunch, the weakened value of the pound is having a negative impact on overseas travel and so impacting on airlines and the travel sector. However some have found opportunities in the economic recession. The UK holiday sector is doing relatively well with a growth in demand for UK holidays, both from local residents and overseas visitors who are benefiting from the weakened pound.

- Similarly within sectors not everyone is impacted equally – in the UK retail sector '*value*' brands like Primark and Pound Shop have expanded and grown whilst Pizza Express has benefited from increased eating at home (compared to other pizza restaurants who do not have any '*at home*' supermarket sold offerings like Pizza Express).

MARKETING AT WORK

Tin manufacturers worldwide benefited from increased demand during 2008 and 2009 as consumers switched from more expensive fresh foods, bottled beers and premium dog food to cheaper canned alternatives. So called '*comfort foods*' such as tinned rice and sponge puddings and baked beans were also purchased as consumers sought their childhood pleasures to increase their feel good factor during the gloomy period.

Tin plate manufacturer Corus increased the price of tin in order to cope with demand during the same period in which manufacturers in many industries moved to shorter working weeks and short term factory shut downs to cope in the economic down turn (Buckley, 2009).

Within a sector those organisations and managers who are aware of their external environment, understand its significance, are alert to emerging trends and themes are most likely to be able to respond to both threats and opportunities generated by a changing business landscape.

This first Unit of your Chartered Postgraduate Diploma is intended to provide you with the knowledge and tools to ensure:

- your planning and marketing activities are based on a realistic assessment of the future environment
- you have tools and skills to help your forecast
- you can take a lead in helping your sector and organisation prepare for future changes
- you are able to be flexible in response to unexpected changes – taking a more **emergent** approach to business planning.

But of course it is not just economic change that drives the fortunes of sectors or organisations. Identifying the macro trends is one thing but the emerging themes are the result of how these changes are acted on by customers, suppliers and competitors. Failing to keep up with this change and these emerging themes is the real cause of failure. So for example the credit crunch is encouraging a pattern of '*thrift*' amongst customers. Avoiding waste and value purchasing are strong emerging themes which may outlive the current economic downturn and need to be reflected in marketing activities and even new business models.

Management guru Gary Hamel says that businesses today are more likely to fail because they become irrelevant, not because they are inefficient. They lose touch with changing customer needs or fail to respond to new competitors who enter the market with new business models. Hamel's (2000) quote from his book **Leading the Revolution** is more graphic but encapsulates the danger of failing to keep abreast of those emerging trends:

"*In today's business environment those who live by the sword shall be shot by those who don't*".

1.2 Strategic wear-out

Failure to respond to the changing environment leads to business failure (strategic wear-out). In fast moving environments there is a real danger of **strategic wear-out.** This occurs when a strategy that has worked well for an organisation previously ceases to be effective. If the organisation fails to notice the changes in the market conditions, becomes complacent and 'sticks to its knitting' it will find business performance falls. The speed of its demise depends on the speed with which its market is changing.

MARKETING AT WORK

application

Bill Gates is described as telling his team '*we are only two years away from corporate failure*'.

Complacency is one of the greatest threats to survival.

There are many instances where products have been replaced. A few recent examples include:

- Digital cameras reduced the need for film development
- MP3 and ipods mean music downloads can replace CD sales
- Movies on demand mean fewer trips to the DVD rental shop
- The Government's smoking ban in public is blamed for the closure of many pubs

The changing fortunes of different sectors can be traced to macro environmental changes that have impacted upon them.

C.K Pralahad and Hamel (1996) highlight the challenges of environmental change, which they point out is creating a growing disconnect between what customers want (driven by changing lifestyles, attitudes and behaviours) and what companies think they want (driven too often by what they can make).

There is a growing disconnect in the exchange process

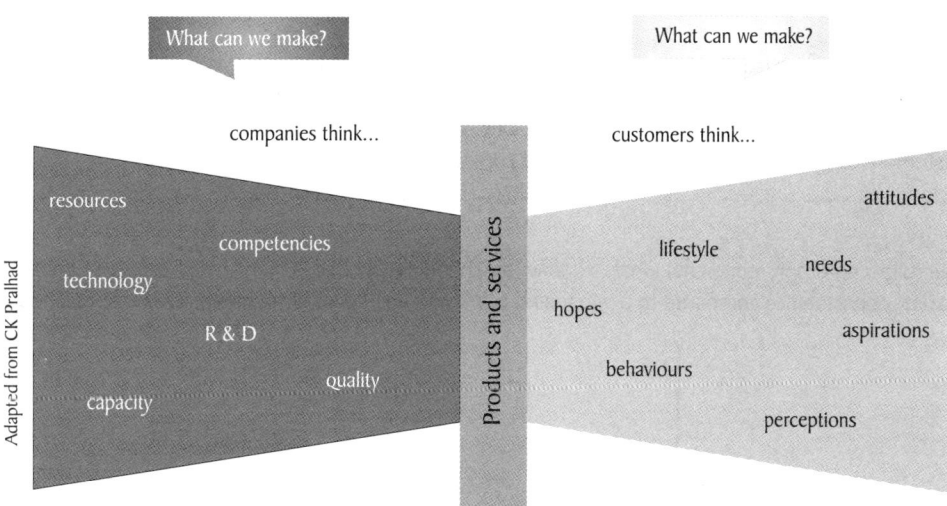

Improved communications and information amplifies any disconnect

According to Prahalad and Hamel (1996) this disconnect is magnified by improved information and communication for customers. Social networks, internet searches and reviews from other users have all contributed to changes in the balance of power in the market place and the creation of buyer markets.

ASSIGNMENT TIP

concept

Note: Changing buyer power is an example of an emerging theme highlighted in the syllabus for this unit. Take a few minutes to consider how buyer power has changed in your sector or industry over recent years and identify what have been the catalysts of this change.

So business takes place in an ever changing environment and recent years have seen the pace of change quicken – new technology, economic collapse, legal and social changes can all be cited as examples of the speed of change. Effective managers therefore have to set up systems to ensure they are alert to emerging changes in their sector. Then they should have the foresight to prepare for them at the organisational level.

2 Change and the planning gap

2.1 But why are these changes so important?

If the external environment was to **stop** changing there would be no external forces driving business performance. As a result you could expect the business to be as profitable tomorrow as it is today. No new technology to improve efficiency, no changes in customer tastes or preferences changing demand, no legal or political shifts impacting on the nature of competition in the sector.

It is the changes in the external environment that generate threats. They can reduce demand, raise costs or erode margins and so determine the bottom line of your planning gap. The planning gap is a forecast of what profits you might expect going forward if you were to *do nothing different* – in other words if you were to keep offering the same products to the same customers despite the changing environment.

This is of course a future forecast of the financial impact of changes in your sector – the result of your awareness of those emerging themes and their potential implications for performance if you fail to respond. Clearly complacency amongst management is not a recipe for success.

 MARKETING AT WORK   application

Woolworths did not fail simply because of the impact of the credit crunch. It had already become **irrelevant** to its customers – people were no longer sure why they should go to Woolworths. The credit crunch simply speeded up the inevitable result of catastrophic strategic wear-out. Woolworths had continued to offer the same products to the same customers despite the changing customer and competitor landscape.

The following graph represents what is known as The Planning Gap. The graph shows the difference between the value of market opportunities compared to a worsening market condition within a relatively stable business environment.

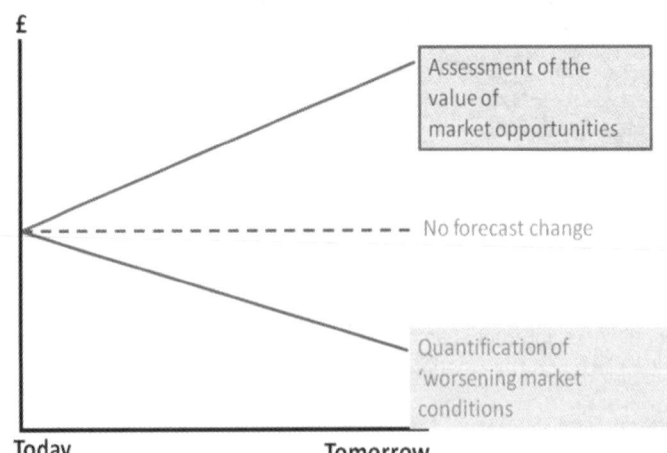

Luckily the changing environment brings with it opportunities as well, providing managers with options to counter the potential downward push from environmental threats. So the top line of the planning gap is a realistic forecast of the potential value of those positive environmental changes if the business was to take advantage of them by responding with new product and marketing strategies.

The planning gap shapes the scope of your **rational** planning. Where are you now, where might you go to and what will happen if you do nothing different. You can see how much business needs to be retained and how challenging your acquisition strategies need to be to take advantage of the emerging opportunities.

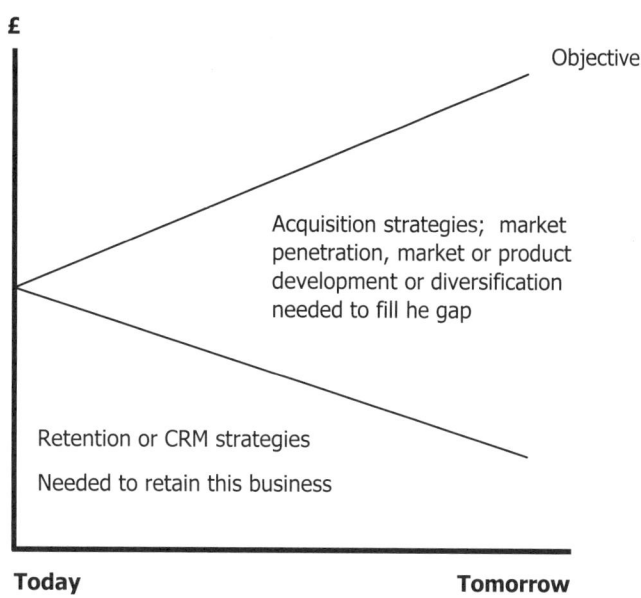

2.2 Where do the opportunities come from?

On its own a change in the environment does not translate into new business. Revenue is generated by selling goods and services to customers – a combination of products and markets. The Ansoff Matrix (below) captures the four strategic options open to an organisation that wants to grow the top line of its business i.e. boost revenues.

	Existing products	New products
Existing markets	Market penetration	Product development
New markets	Market development	Diversification

These strategic opportunities arise from those changes in the environment and how you, your customers and competitors respond to them. So for example a faster pace of life and concerns about work-life balance generate opportunities for time-saving solutions. Examples include prepared meals and ingredients pre-weighed and combined to make home cooked meals easier and quicker.

Even threats in the external environment can be converted into product/market opportunities. Recession may be reducing demand for your premium priced products but it may open up the opportunity for an economy range. Think about the M&S response of a '*dine in for £10 for 2*' offer to attract thrifty shoppers looking for an alternative to an expensive meal out.

In this way external changes in the environment can impact on your expected revenues and margins (positively or negatively) and they can be the catalyst for new business in the form of new customer segments, greater average spend or new products and solutions.

ACTIVITY 2 application

Have a look at the changes in the external environment suggested below. How would you expect them to impact on the organisations in the sectors identified? Think about both margins and how they could become possible opportunities in terms of products and markets.

The shoe industry identifies that there is a steady growth in the average foot size.	
Continued climate change will result in longer, warmer summers in the UK – how might this affect ice cream manufacturers?	
The newspaper industry recognises that more people are getting their news on line	
Latest figures show that dog ownership is in decline but cat ownership is increasing. What are the implications for pet food manufacturers?	
There is evidence that more people are using comparison web sites before purchasing insurance products – how might that impact on motor insurance providers?	
Credit is difficult to get for core SME customers – what are the implications for software suppliers?	
There is evidence that more competitors within a sector are collaborating to gain greater economies of scale	
The credit crunch has boosted the 'stay at home' holiday industry – what are the implications for UK theme parks and entertainment providers?	

You can check your 'forecasts' with ours at the end of this chapter.

2.3 Summarising the underlying challenge

The reason for the emphasis CIM is placing on emerging themes in this qualification becomes clear when you review just how significant those underlying changes are.

It is external (macro-environmental changes) that cause market conditions to change – to respond we need to change: culture, structure and offers.	• Environmental forecasting and flexibility to change are therefore key
These external changes also impact on customers, competitors and key stakeholders and therefore your organisation's fortunes	• Stakeholder mapping & management plus customer insight is crucial
It is therefore critical that we understand these key drivers of change in our sector and appreciate their implications.	• External focus is therefore integral to success.

3 The Business Reality

When you consider the significance of environmental change on performance you might expect forecasting and awareness of emerging themes to be high on management's agenda and the focus of much effort and energy. The business reality is often very different:

- Many organisations produce their business plans without any apparent consideration of the external environment in which they are operating.

- If external factors are considered, they are too often assessed in terms of today's state. This is clearly unhelpful when you consider that we are trying to plan for business tomorrow. In other words it is not the current rate of inflation or customers' attitudes to fast food that matter, it is what we try to forecast these will be in one, two or five years. It is the emerging themes and changes that matter to business fortunes because these are the early indicators of change.

- Forecasting environmental change and future impact is hard and an art not science. However a rational and well thought through, robust approach can be used.

- Few organisations dedicate staff to the monitoring of the environment or take steps to identify and monitor emerging themes. At best the external environment is reviewed superficially as part of the annual planning process and one element of the SWOT analysis.

In truth environmental auditing, or scanning, is a fundamental responsibility of management. Its business plan is needed to steer the organisation through this changing environment over the next 3-5 years.

Failure to audit the environment fully is equivalent to navigating a ship with eyes closed and is likely to result in the business running aground or crashing into something.

 ACTIVITY 3 *evaluation*

Take the business pages from a broadsheet paper or a business magazine like the Economist or Management Today.

Review each of the articles and identify how many of them relate directly or indirectly to a change in the external/macro environment. What is the nature of that change and might it have any impact on the sector you are working in?

3.1 What is an emerging theme?

KEY CONCEPT

concept

Contemporary issues and **emerging themes** are terms used by the CIM to highlight the most potent forces currently influencing sectors of the economy and in turn business practices and marketing strategy. Emerging themes exist where there is some indication of a future change but it is not yet an established factor. The earlier you can accurately identify and factor in such future influences, the more effective your strategy is likely to be.

By definition it is not possible for CIM to be specific about what this year's emerging themes will be – they will change. Two years ago the credit crunch was unlikely to have been on the agenda. Today you might consider the emerging theme to be deflation and the impact that might have on the economy and your markets.

Amongst the potential emerging themes highlighted in the syllabus are:

Political	Devolution and network governance
Economic	Credit crunch
Social	Changing demographics, migration, social networking health and obesity
Technology	Emerging technologies like nano & 3D printing
Environmental	Climate change
Marketing's new ground	Social, green and digital marketing
Changing consumers	Customer power and ethical consumption
Changing nature of competition and supply chains	Collaboration, disintermediation and competition
Contemporary business strategies	Business sustainability and the triple bottom line
The impact on the marketing professional	Intelligence gathering, creative, and flexible thinking

ASSIGNMENT TIP

concept

The CIM has identified the 2012 London Olympics as an emerging theme to feature in marketers' thinking over the next couple of years.

3.2 How things have changed

By taking something of a long view we can see how the changing external environment has impacted on business and the role and activity of marketers.

From a seller's market....

Until 1954 the UK still had rationing, demand exceeded supply and customer choice and the role for marketing were both very limited. Organisations could improve profit if they improved their output so the focus was internal on improving efficiency.

...to a buyer's market

Over time macro environmental change shifted the balance of power:

- Technology reduced barriers to entry in some sectors whilst in others it increased capacity.

- Political changes created a growing single market in Europe and opened up trade with China, both bringing new competitors as well as new customers

- Regulatory changes reduced entry barriers, for example building societies were allowed to compete with banks

- A steady proliferation of media gave customers access to new sources of information.

As these changes took place so the market conditions changed and supply gradually matched and then exceeded demand. The result is a steady change in buyer power creating a theme that has been in evidence for some time!

The role of marketing began to develop, initially as a sales support role with a focus on promotion and communication to more recently (in light of strong buyer markets) to becoming the organisation's architect of competitive advantage. How firms do business and use marketing has changed significantly.

This new strategic role requires marketers to deliver customer insight to the business in ways that help the company decide what benefits will deliver a '*valued offer*' to the targeted segments.

The changing dynamics can be seen in the diagram below. Proliferation of product and media since the 1950's led to this switch from seller's to buyer's market, with the customer now in the driving seat.

Changing market dynamics

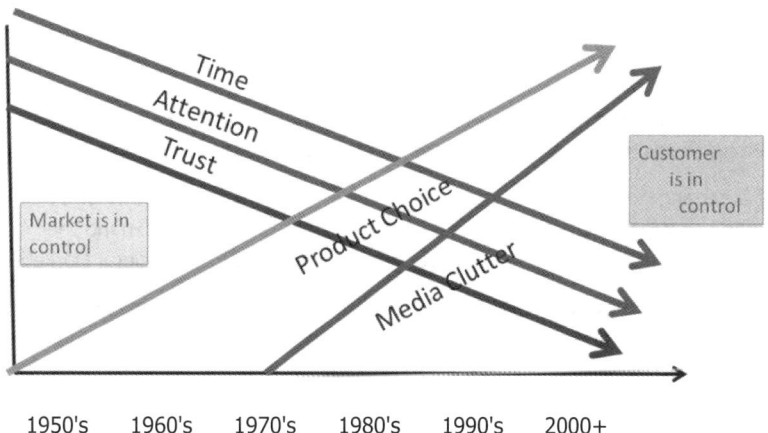

....and the impact of recession

The credit crunch and recession have not reversed the buyer's market. On the contrary reduction in demand magnifies the excess of supply over demand. Not all players will survive so the emphasis is on trying to ensure your organisation is truly market oriented. Companies who have perhaps paid only lip service to customer led decision-making are working very hard to establish a meaningful strategic role for marketing in today's tough economic climate.

KEY CONCEPT

concept

An emerging theme – competition for attention

To date marketers have had to compete for a **share of wallet** and income was a key segmentation variable. Marketers recognised the increased customer choice made possible by a buyer's market. The proliferation of media we are enjoying today will have significant implications for marketers because in future we will also be competing for attention. Permission to communicate with customers cannot be assumed – **time and attention** will be scarce commodities we will need to compete for so therefore **relevance** will become increasingly critical.

ACTIVITY 4

application

The implications

What are the implications of competing for time and attention in your market?

How might your marketing strategies and tactics have to change?

3.3 A broader stakeholder agenda

Whilst many organisations are still coming to grips with the reality of a market orientation there is plenty of evidence of what today's emerging trends around CSR (Corporate social responsibility) will mean to business and the role of marketers.

A number of emerging trends are driving this agenda from climate change to waste, demands for better corporate governance and concerns about society. For companies there is a need to expand their agendas to include the needs of employees, the community and the general public. This is referred to as Societal Marketing or human orientation.

Organisations have to assess their costs and value added in terms of economic, social and environmental impact. Reporting on the **triple bottom line** and making decisions about whether CSR initiatives should be simply a matter for compliance, match industry best practice or be used as a differentiator.

ACTIVITY 5

application

Can you use this model and identify on it which organisations in your sector are using CSR as a differentiator, which are merely compliant and which meet industry good practice?

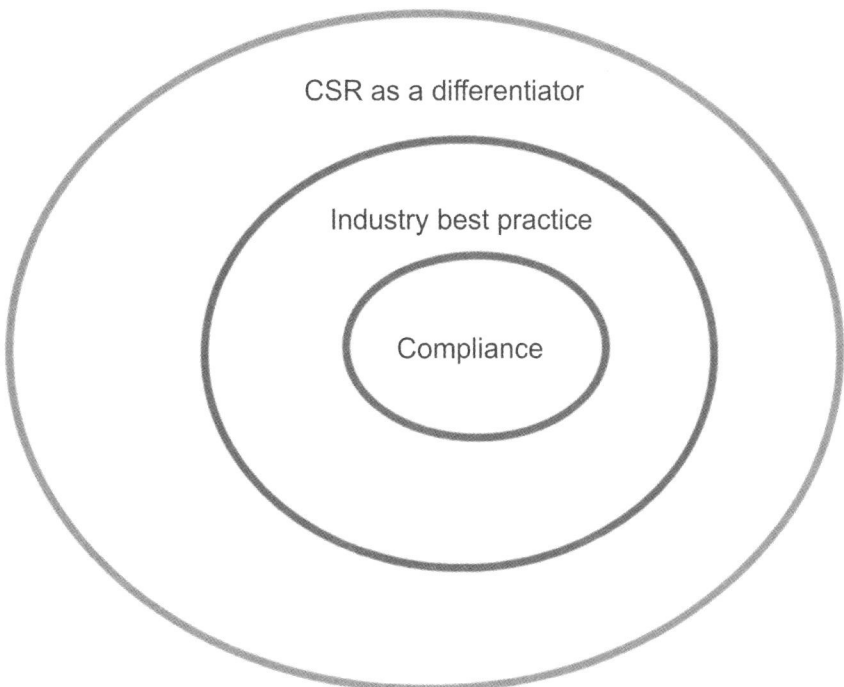

4 An emerging theme

There is a growing sense of distrust. Consumers have been exposed to some critical events recently that have led them to question our social and commercial institutions as well as the brands they buy.

4.1 Corporate Social Responsibility

 MARKETING AT WORK application

Coca Cola's launch of bottled water Dasani which was exposed as being simply filtered Kent tap water. The consuming public is growing ever more suspicious of companies and products.

Stories have ranged from lead-laced children's toys and toxic pet food to corrupt executives. Reckless business decisions have been highlighted. The banking crash of 2008/9 has done little to curb this trend of cynicism.

According to Fitch, a leading retail design consultancy:

- 62% of customers no longer trust everyday social institutions to meet their needs
- over half do not believe brands are interested in improving consumer's lives

Fitch identifies an emerging theme as – '*a shift from carefree to careful consumer*' with a growing demand for companies and brands to demonstrate they are responsible (Fitch, 2009).

The implications for tomorrow's brands may be a rise in brands that '*show their heart beat*' rather more like Innocent and Pret a Manger ('generous' brands).

ACTIVITY 6   evaluation

From *carefree* to *careful*

Is there any evidence of this trend in your sector?

What are/would/could be the implication of this trend for your organisation?

 ## MARKETING AT WORK   application

Plan A because there is no Plan B

In 2001 M&S announced it was only going to sell free range eggs as part of a wider commitment to animal welfare. The operational implications of what you may think was a tactical decision in reality were huge. 4,000 different products were affected and hundreds of suppliers had to make changes in order to become compliant.

The change was promoted with TV ads featuring the live free range hens in shopping trolleys. Measuring the impact of this initiative was harder. It was believed to contribute to M&S regaining the lead over Waitrose as the '*quality*' food provider that year.

M&S also introduced a £200m investment and a 100 point eco plan to become a carbon neutral retailer within 5 years.

There are five pillars that represent the key areas where M&S believes it can tackle the biggest challenges facing it as a retailer. These five areas are:

1. Climate Change
2. Waste
3. Sustainable Raw Materials
4. Health
5. Being a Fair Partner

The credit crunch brought an acknowledgement from CEO Stuart Rose that the plan may be rolled out rather more slowly than first planned, but it was still on the agenda.

ACTIVITY 7

 evaluation

Visit the M&S Plan A site at http://plana.marksandspencer.com/

Assess for yourself the scale of the CSR strategy and the implications it has for the business.

How is the emerging CSR agenda impacting on your sector? What are the opportunities and threats it might generate?

CSR driven opportunities	CSR driven threats

CSR will be a theme that we return to throughout this study text.

Learning objective review

Learning objectives	Covered
1 Justify the need to monitor the macro environment and make changes to strategy as a result	☑ The macro environment is constantly changing. Changes are increasingly rapid. Those changes drive the fortunes of sectors and organisations – generating opportunities and threats.
	☑ Those who fail to respond pro-actively miss the window of opportunity and are likely to experience the irrelevancy of strategic wear-out
2 Critically assess the broad macro environmental factors and how they impact differently on different sectors	☑ PEST/STEEPLE
	☑ The impact on credit crunch for overseas holidays v UK holidays
3 Understand how this environment changes and the nature of 'emerging themes'	☑ The example of health and fitness concerns
	☑ Emerging themes from the credit crunch – thrifty shoppers
4 Be able to explain how environmental changes impact on different sectors and the performance of organisations	☑ The planning gap
	☑ How threats drive the bottom line and opportunities the top line objective
	☑ The danger of strategic wear-out and Gary Hamel's caution about the dangers of irrelevancy
5 Appreciate the resulting changes for strategic marketing and the work of professional marketers	☑ The need for new approaches in response to CSR – the triple bottom line and impact on many aspects of strategy and tactics looking at the M&S example.
	☑ How improved information and communication strengthens buyer power and developments like price comparison websites mean new options for differentiation are needed
6 Have identified how recent environmental changes have impacted on a specific sector.	☑ Throughout this chapter you have been applying the learning to your own sector

Quick quiz

1. What are the key drivers of environmental change?
2. How does the planning gap summarise a sector or organisational level view of the future environmental forecast?
3. What is the triple bottom line?
4. What are the implications of greater buyer power in a market or sector?
5. Do all organisations perform equally well or badly as a result of a sector level change?
6. What is strategic wear-out?
7. What skills are needed within a business to avoid strategic wear-out?

Activity debriefs

1. This will depend on your own research and the journals you refer to. It is an important portfolio building activity for your assignment preparation.

2. These are suggested answers only – you may have generated equally valid alternatives.

Table Title	Table Title
1 The shoe industry identifies that there is a steady growth in the average foot size.	Bigger shoes will use more raw materials and so average costs will increase with a downward effect on margins (unless prices are raised). It creates an opportunity of providing the choice of bigger sizes.
2 Continued climate change will result in longer, warmer summers in the UK – how might this affect ice cream manufacturers?	Sales could be expected to grow so the opportunity for higher ice cream spend per customer (market penetration) and maybe new flavours or distribution channels. Note: The bottom line of the planning gap is upwards in a growth market.
3 The newspaper sector recognises that more people are getting their news on line.	Falling sales through circulation would also lead to lower advertising revenues. Media owners could develop on-line services or may reduce news content in favour of less time sensitive content. Advertisers may force prices down, reducing margins further, or a new business model paying for online content, as implemented by the UK *Times* newspaper, could emerge.
4 Latest figures show that dog ownership is in decline but cat ownership is increasing. What are the implications for pet food manufacturers?	Cat food is probably less profitable (smaller tins) than dog food so although switching resources between the two is an option, it is likely revenues will be reduced – some firms may choose to specialise in cat food provision.
5 There is evidence that more people are using comparison web sites before purchasing insurance products – how might that impact on the motor insurance industry?	This could lead to more commoditisation of the sector, with lower prices reducing average margins. The motor insurance sector will need to compete through price or preferably clear and valued differentiation. Brokers may be replaced by on-line purchasing.
6 Credit is difficult to get for your core SME customers – what are the implications for the software sector?	New pricing models, renting rather than buying software could help by reducing the need for capital outlay. Otherwise sales may fall and there may be less return for the investment in the software development.
7 There is evidence that more of your competitors are collaborating to gain greater economies of scale.	Their average costs will be lower – so they could compete on price, forcing sector prices and margins down. They may also gain control over channels or suppliers which could damage your business – consider joining them?
8 The credit crunch has boosted the 'stay at home' holiday industry – what are the implications for UK theme parks and entertainment providers?	Growth potential. Special family packages and pricing may help as would targeted promotion to ensure UK families consider the park. A penetration strategy is needed.

3. This will depend on the broadsheet you chose.

4–6. Your answers for these activities will be dependent on your own research and the nature of your organisation. Try discussing your answers with colleagues to see if their view is consistent with yours.

7. There are massive implications throughout every department of M&S as a result of Plan A. All areas of the business are likely to be impacted. The impact of CSR is also likely to be large for your own organisation.

Quiz answers

1. The PEST or STEEPLE factors

PEST	STEEPLE
Political and Legal	**S**ocial, cultural and demographic
Economic	**T**echnological
Social, cultural and demographic	**E**conomic and demographic
Technological and environmental	**E**nvironmental
	Political
	Legal
	Ethical

2. The bottom line of the planning gap attempts to put a financial value on the changes that are likely to depress sales and profits whilst the objective set and the top line should be a realistic quantification of the value of emerging opportunities if effectively capitalised on.

3. It refers to reporting business performance in terms of Economic, Social and Environmental impact.

4. Customers have a choice and only firms who respond to their needs can expect to survive.

5. No, they do not always. Some changes, for example legislative or tax change may have an equal impact but others will have different effects depending on the strategy structure and flexibility of the business. So we considered how some retailers were doing better in the recession than others.

6. When a previously successful strategy is past its sell by date. The offer is no longer relevant to changed customer needs and market conditions.

7. External orientation, forecasting skills and customer insight.

References

Buckley, C. (2009) *'Can we survive the recession? Yes we can'* The Times, 23rd March 2009, London.

Central Statistics Office (2009) data available online at www.cso.ie/statistics [accessed 1st June 2009].

Fitch (2009) Corporate website available at www.fitch.com [accessed 1st June 2009].

Hamel, G (2000) Leading the Revolution, Harvard Business School Press, Harvard.

Prahalad C.K. and Hamel, G. (1996) Competing for the Future, Harvard Business School Press, Harvard.

Emerging Themes

Chapter 2
Environmental information

Topic list

1. Which market are we scanning?
2. Establish the macro environmental forces
3. Collecting environmental information
4. Trend analysis
5. Futurology

Introduction

In this chapter we look at the essential task of auditing your marketing environment. This is one of the cornerstones of marketing, and you will have covered it in previous levels of the CIM qualification. We cannot emphasise enough the importance of clear, consistent and methodical analysis.

The chapter begins by considering which market should be scanned. This is not quite as simple as it initially sounds as increasingly organisations span several markets. In order to identify emerging trends, it is vital that focus is clear and sufficiently broad so that relevant opportunities and threats are not overlooked.

The second section moves on to look at macro economic factors. We then look at the information which should be collected and how to apply some of the most commonly used tools in the final sections.

Syllabus linked learning objectives

By the end of the chapter you will be able to:

Learning objectives		Syllabus link
1	Understand the challenges and practical problems associated with environmental scanning and monitoring	1.1
2	Be able to define and scope the 'market' to be scanned	1.2
3	Be able to use a range of methods and tools to help with environmental analysis	1.2
4	Have begun the process of analysis of your sector market	1.2

1 Which market are we scanning?

The problem with analysis undertaken by many organisations isn't the methodology they use but the context and focus of their work. For even a modest SME there are often activities that span several markets and product or solution areas. Any analysis completed at the organisational level will inevitably be vague and only relevant to parts of the business. At too high a level there is little granularity and the lack of focus means it is easy to overlook relevant opportunities and threats and fail completely to identify those emerging trends.

The first challenge for marketers is to define carefully the market they are analysing. That may sound reasonably straightforward but unfortunately it often isn't.

Many organisations still fall into the trap of defining their markets in product terms – we are in the software business or the consultancy market. The problem with this is twofold:

- If you define your business **by what you do** the chances are your orientation will be internal rather than external and those **emerging trends can catch you unaware**.

- Your **customer isn't buying a product but a solution to their problem.** If you fail to recognise this, your definition of competitors and substitute products may well be too narrow. It isn't easy to get a really clear view of what is happening in a market if you approach it with blinkers on (marketing myopia).

1.1 Examples

A CD manufacturer	Your local cinema	The local charity
The customer is buying personal entertainment and is happy to consider new technologies and formats including music downloads	Here the customer is looking for an evening's entertainment and the local theatre, wine bar or tonight's TV programmes are all potential competitors	The competition is for your discretionary pound and your support and empathy

1.2 Mission statements matter

Planning activity and strategy development starts by clarifying the market or business you are in – essentially by defining the mission statement. Do not confuse this with the overall mission statement of the organisation but consider it as the first step in scoping your market. For example, your thinking could start with the phrase:

In this area of our activity we are in the business of providing the following benefits to the following people.

 MARKETING AT WORK application

BPP Learning Media is in the business helping students prepare for and pass professional examinations.

The market can now be defined in terms of those people seeking to prepare for and pass professional exams. Those studying for vocational exams or academic programmes are not in this market. This clarification can help us determine the size of the market and the current and potential competitors who provide any solution to the student's exam passing problem - from direct study text competitors to private tutors and self help study groups.

If you wanted to understand the future of this market you would be looking at the factors influencing demand for professional qualifications and the standards set by the different professional bodies like CIM. An emerging trend towards tougher standards might generate the opportunity for re-sit kits or distance learning tutors.

 ACTIVITY 1 application

Look at the examples given and define their business in terms of the customer benefits being offered or the problem solved, and consider who might be competing in these markets other than the direct competitors.

Firm	They are in the business of	They might be competing with
1 An airline providing internal flights		
2 A manufacturer of plastic carrier bags		
3 A take away pizza restaurant		
4 Your local doctor		
5 The finance team in your organisation		
6 Your own business/organisation		

Check your answers with the feedback at the end of this chapter

> **ASSIGNMENT TIP**
>
> Make sure you are specific about this market definition when preparing for your assignment. Being focused will make life easier for you and will generate more useful insights for your business.
>
> **Warning**
>
> Take care with international markets. Whilst it is quite feasible to have a global market defined as we have done above, your environmental analysis may differ across different geographies. There may be an emerging theme in the Middle East which is not apparent in the Far East. It is of course differences in the external macro environments that makes international marketing so challenging and the extent of those differences will determine how much your strategy has to be adapted to meet local needs.

1.3 The Helicopter Vision

Once you have defined the business you are in, you have the scope for your analysis and can establish the players within that market – other competitors, intermediaries and suppliers.

There are two models that can help you build this helicopter picture:

- Porter's (1979) Five Forces Model
- McDonald and Dunbar's (2004) Market Maps.

1.3.1 Porter's Five Forces

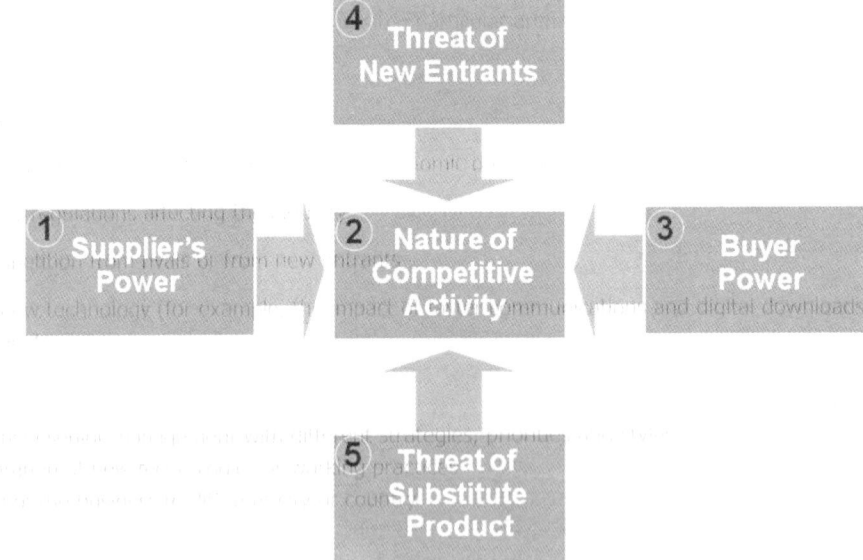

Michael Porter (1979) encouraged organisations to take this helicopter view of their markets, identifying the trends in five specific aspects of their business. Note this is not simply about describing the current situation but forecasting changes in these aspects of the market activity. As you consider each of the Five Forces try and populate a model for your own marketplace.

1. **Supplier power** – consider how Intel used direct appeal to the end user customer to change its power with computer manufacturers. The number and bargaining power of suppliers impacts on margins. What are the emerging trends in the supply side of your business activity?

2. **Nature of competitive activity** – how many competitors are there and how fierce is the competition between them – more significantly how is that changing? Price wars and legislation can be the outcome if competitive activity becomes unbalanced. Governments tend not to approve of markets where there is limited competitive activity.

3. **Buyer power** – this is not just about purchasing power but also about knowledge and information. Over recent years customers across all sectors have become increasingly powerful.
4. **Threat of new entrants** – this is directly related to the barriers to entry and any trends that reduce, or indeed raise, these. New entrants may come from a new sector or new geography.
5. **Threat of substitute product** – this is often linked to new technologies and solutions being developed so trends in technical development need to be watched. Again remember substitutes are any other solution to the same customer problem and in some sectors a DIY option may be a competitor.

ASSIGNMENT TIP

 evaluation

When using models like this, incorporate a traffic light system to help you identify where changes are happening and whether those changes are broadly good for your business or bad.

The Harvard Business Review features an article written by Porter in January 2009 which looks at the Five Forces model in today's world. You can access the article via the CIM's knowledge hub. A link via the HBR to an extract can be found at:

http://hbr.harvardbusiness.org/2008/01/the-five-competitive-forces-that-shape-strategy/ar/1 pg 2

The website of Harvard Business School has excerpts and links to all of Porter's work. It can be found at:

http://www.isc.hbs.edu/

1.3.2 McDonald and Dundar's Market Maps

Market maps are a development of Porter's Five Forces. You can expand on this map to add in suppliers, new entrants and even substitute products. The map below is a simple illustration of the competition for corporate advertising spend and it illustrates how different media owners are getting their solution to corporate customers. You can see the additional detail – particularly in relation to competitive activity, and routes to market that this model offers when compared with the original Five Forces.

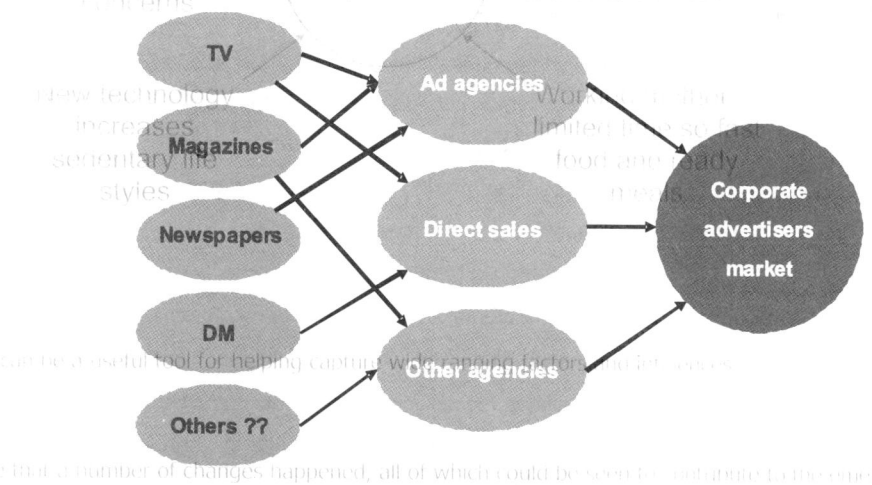

You can capture considerable amounts of information on a map like this, adding in revenues, the percentage of business going through different channels and which competitors are market leaders and followers.

2: Environmental information

Malcolm McDonald and Ian Dunbar (2004) provide a detailed overview of the theoretical and practical uses of market mapping. They look at how to define markets and have useful worksheets to help you work through your own mapping exercise.

2 Establish the macro environmental forces

Once you have defined and scoped your market you can start to identify the external STEEPLE factors that are impacting upon it.

The key here is to be as thorough and specific as possible.

So rather than just talk about '*economy*' it may be the availability of consumer credit that correlates directly to levels of demand. There may be a number of changes that in turn could affect the availability of credit.

Similarly you might have '*employment levels*' as an economic factor, but the true factor may be employment levels amongst 18 – 25 year olds.

Remember also that you are looking always for emerging trends and themes. You may not always be able to be specific about what the '*change*' will be but you may be more certain there *will be* a change. For example a trend for increased legislation in an area, technology breakthroughs or greater policing of internet sites are highly likely to change although we may not know exactly what the change will be.

These environmental changes influence demand and supply. You are therefore looking for factors that directly influence customers and competitors. You can break the process down into two steps, step one involves identifying **drivers** and step two identifying **key trends**.

2.1 Step One – identify key drivers

Start to build up a broad picture of the key drivers using your STEEPLE headings – don't worry about how these are changing at the moment, just consider what are the main factors that have or could influence the market in the future. These then become key factors that you need to set up monitoring processes for.

2.1.1 The market for confectionery and chocolate

The list below is a start at identifying the key drivers in a sector. We have chosen the confectionery market because it is one which many people are familiar with (you could probably add to the issues outlined).

Social & Cultural	–	Attitudes to health and obesity
	–	Attitude to personal indulgences – the '*spoil yourself*' trend
	–	The growth in connoisseur chocolate eating – a little but high quality
Technological	–	New methods of production – safer or longer shelf life
Economic and demographic	–	Demographic profile – chocolate is eaten more by women and the young
	–	Disposable income levels
	–	Pocket money trends
Environmental	–	Issues related to the production of coco products
Political	–	Pressure on the Government to intervene – promoting healthy eating
Legal	–	Legislation re packaging information and advertising to children
	–	European legislation on use of the term 'chocolate'
Ethical	–	Fair trade
	–	Pester power marketing
	–	Encouraging excessive consumption – bigger bars and packets etc

Emerging Themes

ACTIVITY 2 — Drivers

Research application

Try and identify some of the key drivers in a market you are familiar with.

Social & Cultural	
Technological	
Economic and demographic	
Environmental	
Political	
Legal	
Ethical	

2.2 Step Two – Identify trends

Before we look at how you can collect information about the environment we need to consider whether forecasting and trend analysis have a place in such a fast moving world. This was the question addressed in a 2009 article in Marketing Week (Davies, 2009).

'Interpreting Trends' was published on 20 Feb 2009. In the uncertain times resulting from the financial crisis, questions hang over the relevancy of the consumer trends that existed before. This is an interesting article to see how marketers interpret the impact of a range of trends. The article can be found at: www.marketingweek.co.uk/cgi-bin/item.cgi?ap=1&id=64391 - 29k

This article usefully differentiates between fads and trends. It is worth noting that even fads can generate opportunities and threats so still need to be identified and responded to. They may however be more difficult to predict and short-lived in terms of their impact on consumer behaviour.

- **Trends** are grounded in the fundamental forces shaping consumers' lives, capturing important shifts in consumer priorities. The Futures Company have identified Ten Global Energies they believe provide a comprehensive framework to explore the many ways in which consumer and brand behaviour is changing around the world and should have a significant shelf life. Two of these are "Making a Difference" (the green agenda) and 'Seeking Experiences' with customers shifting from demand for products and services to experiences. Such underlying trends are, according to the futures company, likely to survive despite the unexpected events of global financial crisis. You may be seeking more cost-effective experiences if spending is cut, but your expectations are already established by the trend.

- **Fads** however come and go within weeks or months.

- **A bend in the trend?** Ged Davis, formerly head of Scenario Planning at Royal Dutch/Shell is quoted by Davies (2009) in this Marketing Week article. "*a trend is a trend is a trend, until it bends*". It is the bends in the trends that may prove to be the most interesting.

Companies that focus their resources on detecting and acting on these *bends* will be better placed than those who hastily tear up and rewrite their strategies. Abandoning what we understood from the past will not help. Being open, sensitive and responsive to change will determine success.

 KEY CONCEPT concept

You can see that when you are looking at emerging themes you need to give some thought as to whether this is a **trend**, a **bend in a trend** or a **fad** because the strategic importance and implications differ.

 ACTIVITY 3 evaluation

Mintel are forecasting a more entropic society as you can see from the extract below:

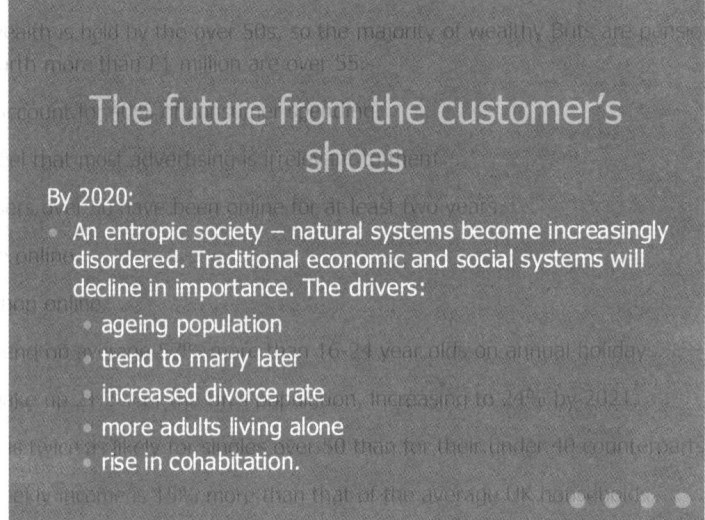

The future from the customer's shoes

By 2020:
- An entropic society — natural systems become increasingly disordered. Traditional economic and social systems will decline in importance. The drivers:
  - ageing population
  - trend to marry later
  - increased divorce rate
  - more adults living alone
  - rise in cohabitation.

Take a few minutes to consider the trend towards a more entropic society.

Take **two sectors** you are familiar with and consider the implications of the underlying trends. Choose which sectors you want but you will find feedback on Social Services and House-building at the end of this section.

Note at this level the examiners are interested in your ability to use a longer time frame when forecasting, and your ability to consider the impact at sector, not just at organisational, level.

Identifying trends starts with you having a sense of the market. What is happening today?

3 Collecting environmental information

Given the potential impact of environmental change on your business performance it is easy to appreciate why businesses ought to be organising themselves to monitor and anticipate sector changes, be they new trends, bends or fads.

In practice few organisations pay as much heed to external monitoring as they do to internal analysis. Those with an external monitoring brief are often scattered across the business. You can find them in business intelligence, corporate planning, research and development and library functions. They are often frustrated by the apparent lack of pro-activity and interest from marketing planners about '*tomorrow's world*'.

There are however a number of methods for collecting environmental information and you may be able to utilise a number of them for your business and CIM assignment.

 ASSIGNMENT TIP application

It is a good idea for you to try to use the following tools to assess your own organisation at the earliest possible opportunity. Once you have your assignment, you will then be in a prime position to start work promptly because you will be aware of the issues of most relevance to your market.

3.1 Market sensing

Market sensing is an approach to monitoring environmental change. It is a technique you already use and indeed may be quite expert in without even recognising it as a technique. It is likely to be particularly useful in establishing emerging trends in your own market.

Market sensing is the result of your own observations and experiences in a market and environment you are familiar with. For example over the last five years in the UK you would have a 'sense of' the increasing concern over obesity in children, the growing 'hostility' towards smokers and the increased interest in governance issues, bankers' pay or politicians' expenses. You will also recognise the '*feel the pinch*' effect of the emerging trend of '*back to basics*'.

Your sense of these and similar trends and themes comes simply from reading the papers, talking to friends, observing the behaviour of others.

The result of this '*market sense*' is that if I was to suggest a new business idea – perhaps a pre-packaged '*at home spa break*' or to take advantage of the demand for '*staycations*' – (economy driven experiences) you would have a '*sense*' of whether this may be an idea worth exploring further.

 MARKETING AT WORK application

Note: One of the biggest challenges for the international marketer comes because they lack the '*sense*' of the overseas market and its customers' behaviour. That sense of a promotions appeal or the suitability of packaging is not there and as a result it is easy to make some culturally naïve marketing decisions.

It is at the micro level of a market – that *bends*, *trends* and *fads* will first be found. To capture this The Future Company employs a network of Global '*Streetscapers*' who are connected to their own culture and networks and so can act as a '*sensing mechanism*' (Davies, 2009).

3.2 Industry level sensing

This '*sensing*' activity takes place at different levels. The manager who has worked in the sector for twenty years has a real 'sense' of the market. What can look like 'gut feel' pronouncements may in fact be quite well homed sensing skills at work.

If you work in pharmaceuticals you will probably be aware of changes in the NHS approach to procurement, have a sense of changing clinical priorities and how major reports like Darzi are influencing the organisation of health care. In this sector the pathway's themes may become an established trend or a change of government policy could leave it as a short lived fad.

In some companies specialist researchers may be briefed to monitor the various sources of industry information, attending events, seminars etc to formalise the 'industry sense'.

Alternatively you may informally provide feedback mechanisms and briefings to encourage your sales teams and client facing staff to act as company '*Streetscapers*'.

 An online article in The Times described how to predict the future for your company. The article can be found at: http://business.timesonline.co.uk/tol/business/career_and_jobs/article5033398.ece

4 Trend analysis

Whereas '*sensing*' may start off as broadly qualitative and based on observation, trend analysis adds to it the qualification and evidence of a pattern over time.

- The climate is getting warmer and summers wetter with average temperature changes of x and rainfall of y compared with 10 years, 50 years or 100 years ago

- People are spending considerably more per annum of their incomes on entertainment. There is a trend for people to marry later, with the average age having risen from x to y.

The problems with trend analysis occur if you simply assume that the trend will continue with no bends. Trends have a life cycle so the pace at which a trend is happening can change and indeed the trends may cease.

Trends could be identified from your own internal sales and customer data.

- For example a trend to sell more eco friendly models.

Increasingly external analysts and specialists are used:

- Organisations like The Futures Company and Mintel provide trend reports and there are briefings services like U talk Marketing and of course CIM White papers etc.

 ASSIGNMENT TIP  application

The challenge for you is to review some of the key sources of trend data available to you and choose those most relevant, accurate and reliable. Remember to keep focused on your market. There may be plenty of interesting information about 16-25 year olds but if your target audience is the over 60's you need reports that focus on the '*greys*'. You won't be short of data but you could end up swamped by it if you aren't clear about your scope and area of interest.

4.1 Expert forecasts

Because tomorrow may be very different from today, those trends may indeed bend. You need to also take a fresh look at tomorrow's markets and what they may look like.

Forecasters in their various guises are '*experts*'. They may be experts in the industry, some aspect of the technology development or the customer. Their expertise gives them added credibility when they consider the '*picture*' shape of the market or evolving customer behaviour. Consider the example of weather forecasters.

An expert would be someone like Bill Gates. His forecasts about the intelligent house of the future are worth listening to.

Experts can often be heard at industry events or they may be academics publishing research papers and writing articles. Their views are however the views of individuals and so should be taken into consideration alongside other sources of information.

4.2 Jury forecasts

Jury forecasts are generated by a group of people who usually have knowledge of, or experience of, the sector or market. It could be as simple as your own management team pooling ideas and insights about changes in the market place.

Alternatively you can convene a jury specifically to review and discuss this topic. You may choose representatives or suppliers and customers as well as your own team. Well facilitated group discussions like this can generate considerable output and jurors can come to a consensus view about many issues.

ACTIVITY 4 — application

You may like to try this yourself. Set up a '*jury*' at work drawn from colleagues or at home with friends and family. If you don't want to focus on your own market set an agenda others can contribute to. The changing market for out of home entertainment or future trends in healthy lifestyles are possible topics.

What are the emerging themes?

The problems with the jury forecast include:

- Having to get a group of people together at a specific time.
- The potential for one person to dominate and bias the group view.
- The danger of '*group think*'. Because individuals are not responsible for the outputs, the group becomes rather more radical in its views than the individuals would be.

4.3 Delphi Oracle

The Delphi Oracle addresses some of the shortcomings of jury forecasts. This method allows you to select a diverse group of 'experts' who never meet, and so can come from different locations and sectors, disciplines or backgrounds. It usually utilises a number of stages.

Stage 1   This group agrees to take part in the process.

Stage 2   Each is sent a questionnaire with a lot of open questions that prompt participants to consider aspects of the future nature of markets and customer behaviour.

Stage 3   The results are consolidated and sent out to those involved, who are invited to comment, elaborate or amend their responses in light of the collective opinion. This stage can go on for a number of 'rounds' as the group moves towards a broad consensus.

Because they do not meet a Delphi Oracle group does not get easily dominated and individually take responsibility for their responses.

4.3.1 What the experts say

Management guru Gary Hamel (2000) is dismissive of any notion of forecasting. He points out that organisations can very easily fall into the trap of coming to a single view of how the future will be and then planning for that single future. When things do not pan out as forecast the strategy fails.

Instead, Hamel (2000) talks of organisations developing **foresight** – the notion of them trying to look ahead, being alert but not kidding themselves they can see the future.

In agreement with Arie de Geuse (1997) (who was planning director at Shell), Hamel (2000) promotes the benefits of scenario planning.

Scenarios are set up on the basis of alternative views of the future: what if this happens but what if that happened?

The following diagram summarises the associated process.

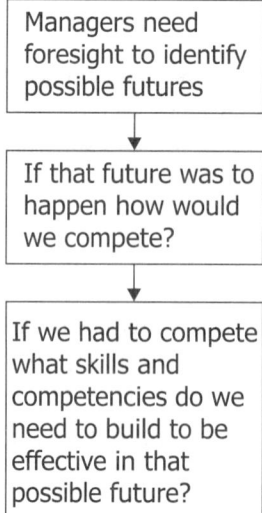

5 Futurology

Finally in our list of methods for considering the future there is *futurology*. A number of organisations, particularly in fast moving technology-based sectors, employ futurologists.

 KEY CONCEPT concept

So what is **futurology**?

It is both an art and a science and some companies are taking it very seriously. It is based on putting forward possible and probable views of the future – it works with the patterns from trend analysis but also incorporates expert understanding and technology insights.

 MARKETING AT WORK application

Take a trip down BT's timeline

BT's futurology department has gazed into the future to predict the technological advances that will impact on our lives.

The timeline encompasses all areas of life influenced by technology developments including artificial intelligence, health and medical, business and education, demographics, energy, robotics, space, telecommunications and transport and travel. It predicts:

- By 2012, children could be entertained by video tiles in the bath before sitting in a playroom with wallpaper which changes to promote energy, happiness or calm. And they could even be interacting with toys that respond to their voices with matching emotions.

- BT predicts we could be holidaying somewhere above the earth's surface by 2017.

- By 2040, the timeline predicts we could get a space elevator to take us up to a moon village that will have developed by then.

BT researcher and editor of the timeline Ian Neild said: "The timeline enables organisations to design technology and products with future customers in mind, with a vision of the kind of environment they will be living in.

"Looking at the future of education or lifestyles, for example, will impact the way BT enhances and develops its broadband network."

The BT futurology team looked at both personal and professional scenarios when compiling the timeline.

It is worth a visit. Take their interactive tour, but with a purpose. Choose at least one of their predictions and consider how it would have an impact on your sector and what you might say if asked to brief a number of companies in your sector about this change.

(Source: http://www.btplc.com/innovation/news/timeline.htm)

5.1 Making sense of the changes

Once you have completed your environmental analysis you need to *'sort'* the factors identified.

You need to treat opportunities and threats differently to avoid confusing them later.

For each category and factor you want to consider:

- the likelihood that it will happen
- the significance to the business if it does.

5.1.1 Opportunity/threat matrix

	Very likely	Likely	Less likely
Very significant	Plan	Contingency Plan	Scenario Plan
Significant	Plan	Monitor	Reject
Less significant	Monitor	Reject	Reject

(To happen: Very likely / Likely / Less likely — Significance to the business: Very significant / Significant / Less significant)

Produce a separate **opportunity and threat matrix** and use the matrix to help you identify which you must build into your plan.

- **Plan for the '*likely*'** or that which will probably that have a significant impact
- Factors which would be significant to your forecast but are not confirmed events require **contingency plans**. You are already an expert contingency planner – it is a normal approach to planning. If it is likely to be a nice day and you are having friends round you might plan to have a barbecue. The weather is, of course, a very significant factor in this decision, so you may have a contingency plan in case there is an unexpected rainstorm.
- The unlikely, but significant, factors can be the focus of **scenario plans** – '*what would we do if?* As individuals many of us have scenario plans in case we win the Pools or the National Lottery - unlikely, but it would have a significant impact on our lives. Some organisations have followed the lead of Shell, who developed scenario planning as a technique for improving planning skills amongst their managers.

MARKETING AT WORK

application

It is reported that Shell was the only company prepared for the first Gulf War. It had scenario plans based on terrorists closing one-third of the world's oil fields. Pre-thinking on rationing, alternative sources and handling customers would have given them considerable competitive advantage had the war dragged on. It seems likely that very few organisations had scenario plans for a significant recession – despite the fact that there is a history not just of trade cycle activity but of a pattern of serious downturns every 50 or so years.

5.2 Scenario planning

Scenario planning is particularly useful when addressing the question of emerging themes. They allow you the chance to consider not just a single forecast future but a number of alternative futures and so assess the implications and potential impact on your industry and sector and how an individual organisation might need to respond if it is to compete effectively.

Using sector analysis

Changing consumer behaviour and food retail

The seven emerging trends shown in the diagram below are taken from work done by a major food retailer in the UK in 2008. Take a minute to review them and consider them in the context of your own personal shopping habits. The '*Do It For Me Trend*' may be reversed somewhat by the credit crunch – have you started washing your own car or buying less ready-made meals?

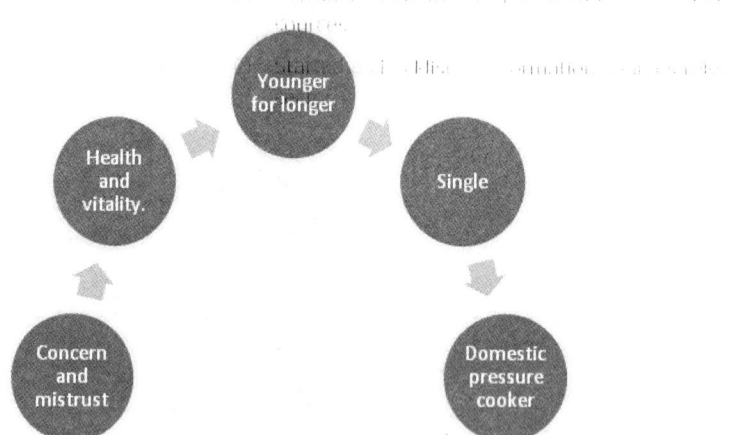

1. Is it important to be able to map the sequence of inter-related changes in the environment?
2. Should the marketing professional treat all emerging themes the same?
3. How might Force Field Analysis help you assess an emerging theme?
4. On a Force Field map what would different thicknesses of arrows indicate?
5. What is a restraining force in Force Field Analysis?
6. Why is Porter's Five Forces model useful in your analysis?
7. What sources of information may be available to support your analysis?

If you were advising a food retailer on the implications of these changes on marketing mix activities what would you be considering? How might the mix need to change going forward?

Marketing mix	Implication
Product development	
Promotion	
Pricing	
Distribution	
Physical evidence	
Processes	
People	

You can compare your ideas with the feedback at the end of this chapter.

Learning objective review

	Learning objectives		Covered
1	Understand the challenges and practical problems associated with environmental scanning and monitoring	☑	Buy in
		☑	Many approaches
		☑	Bends vs trends vs fads
2	Be able to define and scope the 'market' to be scanned	☑	Marketing myopia
		☑	Mission statements
		☑	Difficulties with international markets
		☑	Helicopter vision
3	Be able to use a range of methods and tools to help with environmental analysis	☑	Sensing
		☑	Trend analysis
		☑	Futurology
4	Have begun the process of analysis of your sector market	☑	Activities throughout the chapter

2: Environmental information

Quick quiz

1. Why is it sometimes difficult for marketers to identify their market?

2. Customers always buy solutions to problems. True or false?

3. Porter's Five Forces model is used to:

    a. describe the current situation for an organisation

    b. only look at entire industries

    c. look at the current market and forecasting future changes

4. Market maps developed from Porter's Five Forces. True or False?

5. STEEPLE factors are considered:

    a. as an initial stage of analysing the market

    b. once the market scope has been defined

    c. at any time so long as it is completed

6. Fads:

    a. come and go within weeks or months

    b. are long-lasting and likely to sustain short-term challenges

    c. should lead to a strategy renewal

7. What is the difference between sensing and trend analysis?

8. What is the difference between an expert forecast and a jury forecast?

Activity debriefs

1.

Firm	They are in the business of	They might be competing with
1 An airline providing internal flights	Transporting people and goods over medium distances, quickly and safely	Railways, cars and video conferencing
2 A manufacturer of plastic carrier bags	Providing disposable and cheap solutions for packaging and transporting goods	Natural fibre bags and reusable carrier bags, boxes and alternative packaging
3 A take away pizza restaurant	Providing customers with the option of not cooking	Restaurants, other take away food providers and 'easy to make' pre-prepared food dishes.
4 Your local doctor	Keeping you well and if sick helping you recover quickly	Alternative therapists and DIY or over the counter remedies as well as the temptations that might discourage you from a healthy lifestyle
5 The finance team in your organisation	Providing managers with accurate and timely financial analysis and information to support improved decision making	Gut feel decisions and DIY financial analysis.
6 Your own business/organisation	(remember what benefits to whom)	

2. Your answer will depend on your own organisation.

34 Emerging Themes

3 An example of two sectors is shown below. Your answer may depend on the industries you chose.

Social services	House-building
Greater demand for services to support both the elderly and children from broken homes or living with single parents	Demand for features that support independent living for longer – wheelchair access and technology to aid everyday tasks
New methods of social support needed – communities and virtual support groups to keep costs low	Flexible property units to allow additional modules to be added as family sizes change – older children staying or returning home and single parents cohabiting and merging families
Less obvious authority sources may mean social unrest, crime and threats to the officers of the public sector increase	Greater interest in security features and community spaces to deal with isolation problems
More 'nannying' culture as the State tries to fill in the gaps left by the breakdown of more traditional family networks	

4 Your answer will depend on both the trend you are considering and also the make up of the 'jury'.

5 We have used the example of food retailing and how it is likely to be impacted by trends.

Marketing mix	Implication
Product development	Single portions, additive free ingredients, more organic and sustainable sources. More pre-combination of ingredients making 'cooking from scratch' easier. Increased customisation – my curry ingredients will reflect my preferences
Promotion	Ethical and honest – demands for transparency of sources Promotions that reward loyalty
Pricing	Single portions may yield higher overall profits but lower average spend per customer. Loyal customers will want value for money
Distribution	Convenience matters – delivered to home (internet purchases) or local outlets to help reduce the pressure cooker effect
Physical evidence	Less packaging overall but information with products will be important
Processes	There will need to be processes in place so the source of food products, organic, fair-trade etc can be demonstrated to customers
	I expect to be a valued customer – my preferences will be known and respected
People	The face of the organisation may be increasingly important if we do not trust brands – the Jamie Oliver effect may be more reassuring

Quiz answers

1. Because activities within organisations often span a number of industries, products and solution areas.
2. True. People do not buy lightbulbs for their own sake but so that they can see in the dark. Remember the differences between features and benefits.
3. C. It is also used to help with market forecasting.
4. True. Maps add additional detail to the Five Forces model.
5. B. You cannot identify STEEPLE factors until you have identified the scope of the market they are likely to impact.
6. A. Fads are short term whilst trends are more longer lasting.
7. Sensing is broadly qualitative and based on observation. Trend analysis adds to the quantification and evidence of a pattern over time.
8. Experts in the industry, technology or customer are often speakers at conferences and write articles enabling their views to be disseminated. The view however is of just one individual. Jury forecasts on the other hand involve a group of 'experts' who can debate their views.

References

Davies, S. (2009) *"Interpreting Trends"* Marketing Week, 20th February 2009, London.

de Geuse, A. (1997) The Living Company, Harvard Business School Press, Harvard.

Hamel, G (2000) Leading the Revolution Harvard Business School Press, Harvard.

McDonald, M. and Dunbar, I (2004) Market Segmentation: How to do it – how to profit from it, Elsevier, Oxford.

Porter, M (1979) "*How competitive forces shape strategy*" Harvard Business Review, Harvard.

Chapter 3
Evaluating and assessing emerging themes

Topic list

1. Drivers of change
2. The response to drivers
3. Sector implications
4. Using Porter's Five Forces

Introduction

So far we have been looking at macro changes and their impact in isolation. In this chapter we will be considering the reality of how complex environmental changes are. We shall also examine how many changes and themes may be the result of several separate but aligned changes elsewhere in the environment.

Syllabus linked learning objectives

By the end of the chapter you will be able to:

Learning objectives	Syllabus link
1 Map how a range of changes may bring about emerging themes.	1.1
2 Be able to use Kurt Lewins's force field analysis and Porter's Five Forces to help assess the strength of changes and help evaluate which should be acted upon.	1.2
3 'Forecast' how macro level changes might impact upon different sectors.	All syllabus
4 Use a **variety** of sources.	All syllabus

1 Drivers of change

  concept

Change drivers identify the need or desire for change in a particular area.

They include:

External events

- Changes in the economic cycle (for example, an economic downturn)
- New laws or regulations affecting the industry
- Stiffer competition from rivals or from new entrants
- Arrival of new technology (for example, the impact of faster communications and digital downloads on music and film entertainment)

Internal events

- Arrival of new senior management with different strategies, priorities and styles
- Implementation of new technologies or working practices
- Relocation of the business to different city or country

So far we have looked at change examples in isolation. Many of them have been highly observable, for example the impact of the credit crunch or concerns about fitness and obesity.

In reality this is something of a simplification. Many emerging themes are not the result of a single change but perhaps several changes that coincide. Unravelling the sequence of change and the cycle of cause and effect can be particularly challenging and may in terms of a 'time line' be of little help to the marketer.

However the real challenge is not analysing what has already happened but trying to forecast changes that are still perhaps in their embryonic stage. How can you identify which changes need to be taken seriously and built into your scenario plans and which can be rejected as having no significant long term implications?

How for example might the emergence of online activities like Twitter impact on tomorrow's marketing practices. Similarly how might the re-emergence of 3D technology for cinema spin off different ways of presenting and communicating to customers?

We have already raised the question of today's thrifty customer, a product of the credit crunch and media coverage of it. The question marketers need to address is whether '*thrift*' is an emerging theme, likely to be with us long after the green shoots of recovery or a relatively short term '*fashion fad*'. In Chapter 1 you reviewed the use of opportunities and threats matrices to help you assess the likelihood of change in terms of the impact on your sector or organisation. Here we are taking a more detailed look at assessing the likelihood of an emerging theme becoming a more '*permanent*' change.

1.1 The factors causing a macro environmental change

In practice a number of factors or developments may come together at the same time to create the environmental change.

1.1.1 Example: Drivers of obesity in children

To illustrate this we can look again at the health and obesity issue for children.

First look at the changes coming together that have created the problem. These could be seen to be the emerging themes leading to problem of health and obesity in children.

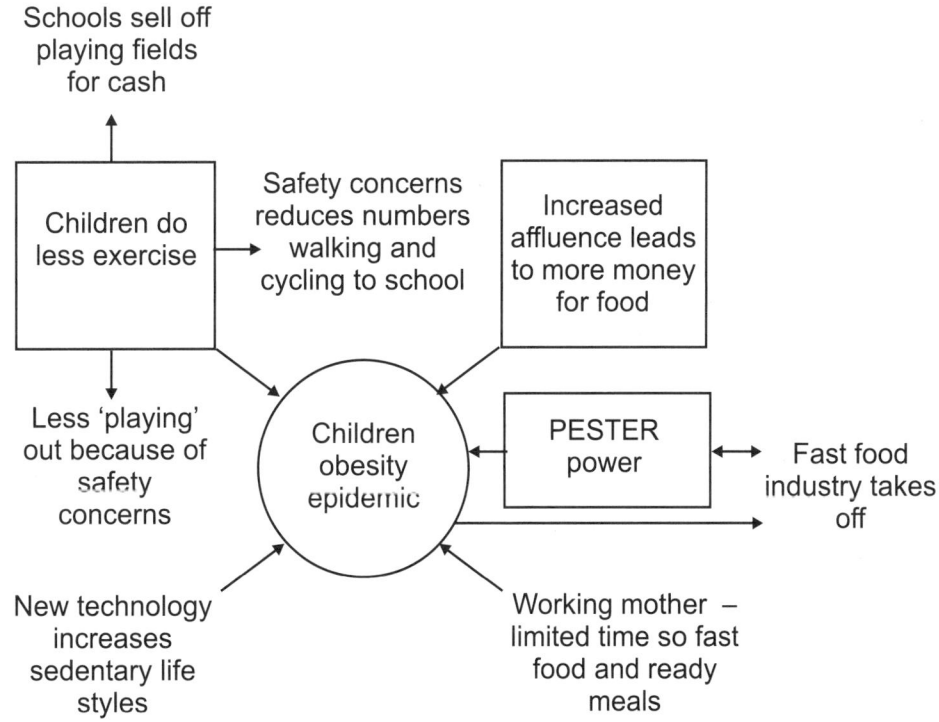

ASSIGNMENT TIP

application

Mind maps can be a useful tool for helping capture wide ranging factors and influences.

You can see that a number of changes happened, all of which could be seen to contribute to the emerging theme of childhood obesity.

These contributing factors range from changes in school funding and governance that allowed school playing fields to be sold through to unnecessary fears about child safety that encouraged families to drive kids to school (aided by the greater affluence and the two car family).

New products and services from games to fast food encouraged less activity and more calories. At the same time children's power grew. At home pester power and at school the '*choice*' in school dinners led to the '*chicken twizzler*', condemned by UK celebrity chef Jamie Oliver for its awful nutritional profile.

So if you were a children's clothes manufacturer or a marketer working in the fast food sector how easy would increasing waist lines of children have been to forecast?

Perhaps more importantly now child obesity is on the agenda how is it likely to change things going forward? What will be the sector responses and the impact on marketers and marketing?

2 The response to drivers

Tackling obesity is a real issue. The UK government (and many overseas governments) are taking it very seriously. They are concerned about the implications on health and costs of the health service. They are using public health marketing to encourage families to be more active, legislating to improve nutritional information on food packaging and in restaurants and encouraging schools to re-engage young people in physical activity.

 MARKETING AT WORK   *application*

The activity involved in Wii games is an example of how identifying a new emerging theme '*getting children fitter*' creates a product opportunity. At the same time Jamie Oliver took the problem as a focus for his school dinners programme. As a crusader for change his response was itself a catalyst for significant change in the provision of school dinners.

So will fitter and less overweight children be the new '*emerging macro level trend*'?
To help us assess the various factors influencing this we need to take a look at the whole picture.

2.1 Force field analysis

Kurt Lewin's (1943) force fields analysis is a tool more normally associated with helping understand and implement change.

We are using it here to help us turn an overview of the '*emerging theme*' and factors driving it into more specific analysis that could help us to evaluate the likelihood of change happening and therefore how seriously the sector needs to take it.

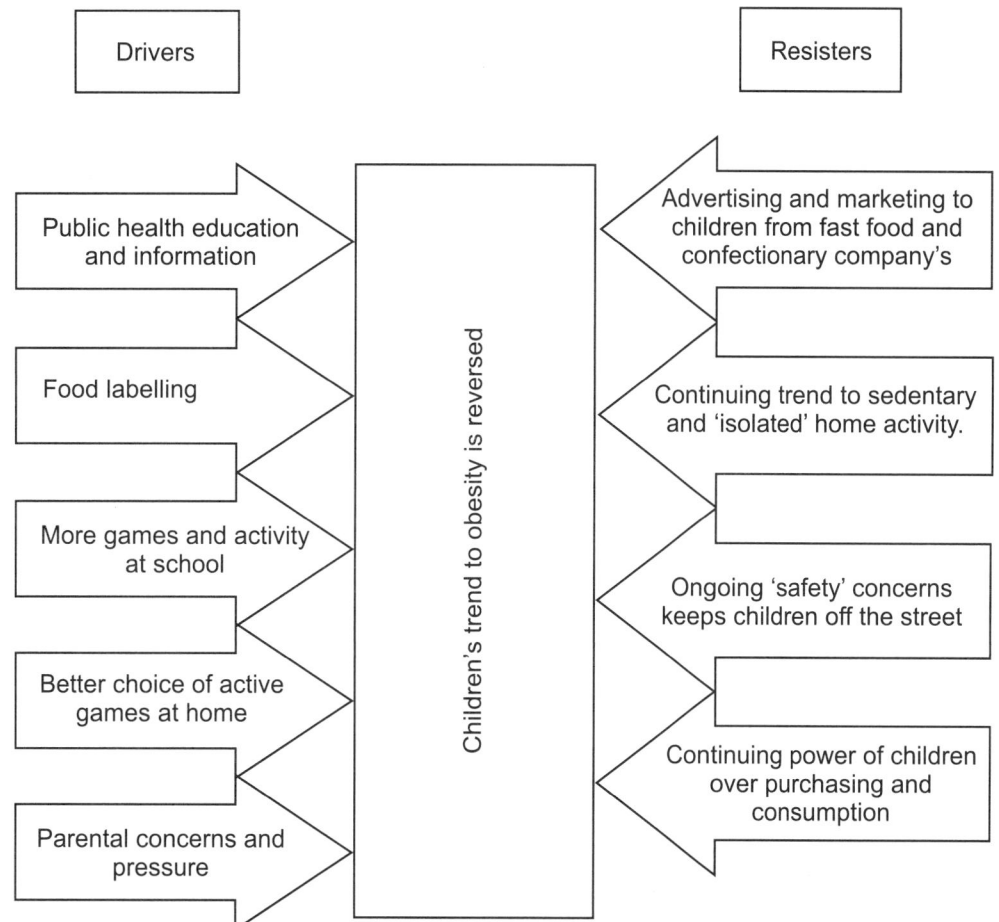

Once you have pulled your analysis together you will be in a better position to judge the relative strengths of the drivers and resistors of change.

ASSIGNMENT TIP · application

Note that you can change the thickness of arrows to indicate difference in the strength of different factors coming to bear on this theme.

2.2 Example: The ageing population

We can use a second theme, the ageing population, to take a look at the themes that are or may emerge and how different changes interact to strengthen (or weaken) an emerging theme/trend.

ACTIVITY 1 · application

The case of the older consumer

Take ten minutes or so and create your own mind map of factors which are driving the trend towards a more active and important older consumer – the growth of the grey market or grey pound.

You can compare your mind map with ours at the end of the chapter.

3: Evaluating and assessing emerging themes

You can see from the activity that the core demographic change is that fact we have an ageing population. The trends are clear in the statistics

- By 2020 over half the population in the UK will be over 50.
- By 2016, 7 million will be over 60 (18% of the population) and 2.6 million over 80

(Source Office of National Statistics, 2009).

More 'older' customers makes them increasingly attractive to business. Their needs and interests become an increasing priority for marketers. As customers, this age group, who have been traditionally rather '*hidden in the wings*', have begun to move centre stage.

Public images of Tina Turner and Mick Jagger turning 60 are illustrations of the '*younger for longer*' theme emerging from this ageing population trend.

Their potential attractiveness to marketers and their growing 'power' is also clear in some of the statistics – as a group their profile makes surprising reading.

The 50-plus target group has remained underestimated for years. Today it is clear that this is the fastest growing segment of the population, with the greatest purchasing power and the most leisure time, and avid for useful information.

- 80% of the UK's wealth is held by the over 50s, so the majority of wealthy Brits are pensioners – more than two thirds of people worth more than £1 million are over 55.
- And the over 50s account for 40% of consumer spending.
- 86% of over 50s feel that most advertising is irrelevant to them.
- 95% of internet users over 50 have been online for at least two years.
- 1/3 of over 50s are online.
- 60% of over 50s shop online.
- 45-54 year olds spend on average 57% more than 16-24 year olds on annual holidays.
- Women over 45 make up 21.2% of the UK's population, increasing to 24% by 2021.
- Sex on a first date is twice as likely for singles over 50 than for their under 40 counterparts.
- 50-60 year olds' weekly income is 15% more than that of the average UK households.
- 50-64 year olds spend 28% more on motoring, leisure goods and services per week than the average UK household.

(Statistics sourced from Office For National Statistics)

It is important that your analysis is supported by data and information drawn from a variety of sources. It isn't good enough to have '*a feeling* older customers are increasingly important.

2.3 And we want them to do more

With greater age tends to come greater social and health costs. Public policy wants/needs this age group to remain independent for as long as possible. In fact with the workforce shrinking relative to the total population they would ideally like them to remain economically active for as long as possible. The result is a '*trend* of policy changes to support this at the top level, including anti age discrimination legislation and changes in retirement age. Amongst the more tactical changes are benefit entitlements intended to support older people living in their own homes for as long as possible.

The interest in, and government support for, independent living in turn stimulates business to fund technological solutions to the limitations caused by age – from mobility scooters to help alert systems. The increasing awareness of how a healthy lifestyle can keep a person '*younger for longer*' is reinforced by another element, rising NHS costs.

Prevention of ill health starts to gain an increasing share of public attention and the public purse.

The emerging themes become apparent:

- People stay younger for longer
- The '*grey*' customer takes centre stage

- Healthier lifestyles
- Ageing but able

These changes and developments create a self-fulfilling prophecy. Happier, respected, occupied, healthier and able people will live longer.

2.3.1 Forecast

It is not just that there are more people over 60 but those people are on average living longer. It is forecast that of the population born today a small, but growing, proportion can expect to live to celebrate 110 birthdays.

ACTIVITY 2   evaluation

Age friendly marketing

These various factors and changes are leading to an emerging theme, '*age friendly*' marketing activity – from the size of type on packaging to the accessibility in stores and entertainment space. You could use Force Field analysis to help you assess the strength of this emerging theme.

Driving   Restraining

Age friendly marketing

3 Sector implications

Having identified the emerging themes we need to address ourselves to the questions of what this means at sector level.

The implications and the relevance of any emerging theme will vary, as we have seen by sector and organisation.

 ACTIVITY 3   evaluation

Take a few minutes to consider the ageing population example and think about the implications for the different sectors highlighted below.

Sector/ Industry	Implications and industry level issues or responses
NHS	
Insurance	
Grocery retail	
Leisure services	
Manufacturers of consumer durables	
House builders	
Your own sector	

You can check your thoughts with ours at the end of this chapter.

4 Using Porter's Five Forces

We considered the use of the Five Forces model in Chapter 1. It can be a very useful model for helping you get a '*snapshot*' helicopter view of a specific sector. Porter's (2008) model encourages a rational approach to strategy planning.

We can use it in the context of one of our emerging themes.

ACTIVITY 4

application

Using Five Forces analysis what conclusions would you draw about changes in the future health care provision for the over 60's?

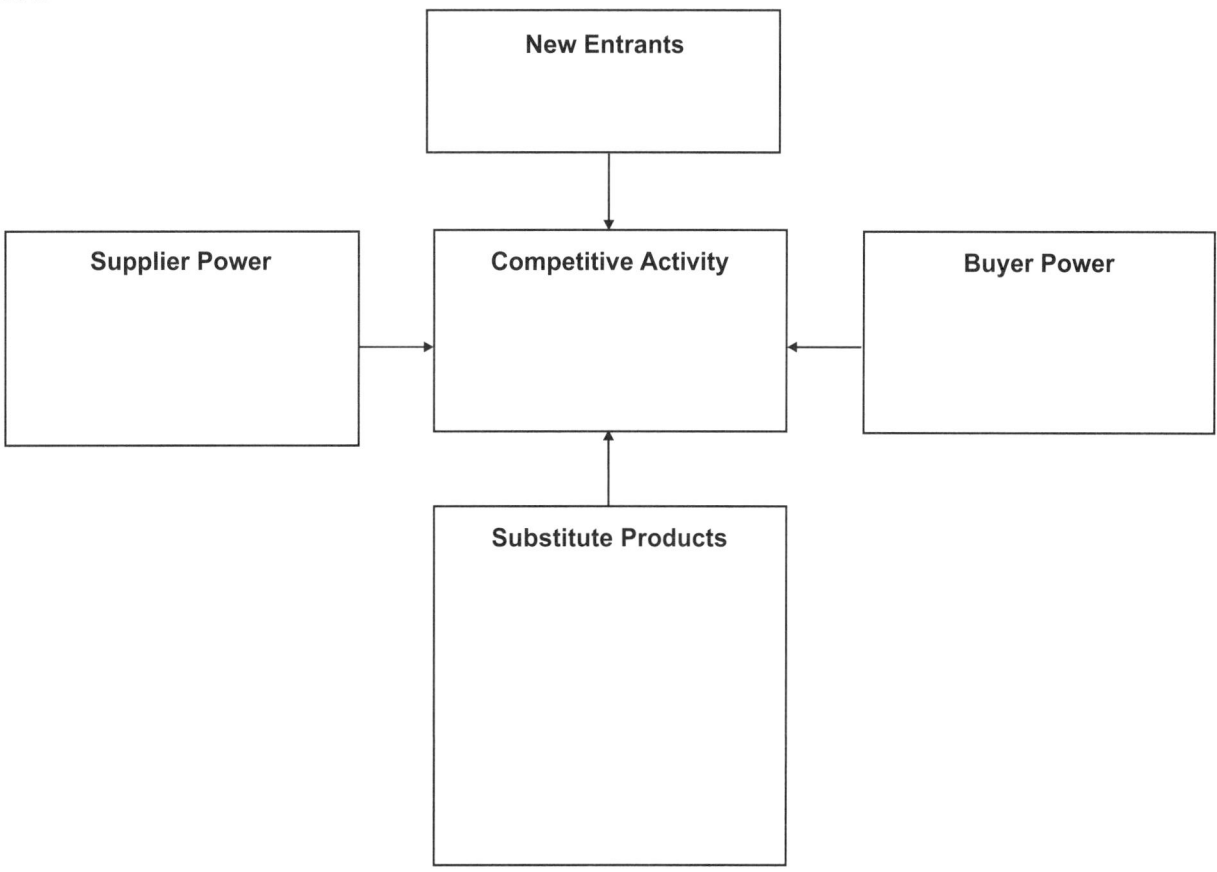

You can compare your assessment with ours at the end of this chapter.

4.1 Sources of information

In order to use Porter's (2008) analysis and to assess the importance and relevance of an emerging theme to your sector you need to have information.

At the heart of this unit is CIM's desire for strategic marketers to be confident in their ability to identify, access and assess data and information from a variety of sources.

This will be the cornerstone of your work on the assignment for this module. Sources of information need to be varied to help you get the fullest view and scope the attitudes of a range of stakeholders and commentators. These should come from business and non business sources.

ASSIGNMENT TIP

application

Start a checklist of information sources relevant to your own industry sector.

ACTIVITY 5

application

Using you own sector and experience create a top line list of the sorts of sources you might be able to call upon.

Check your list with ours at the end of this chapter.

4.2 Assessing your sources

Of course not all of these sources are equally useful, nor indeed can their content be assumed to be equally credible and relevant. You will need to be critical of the information sources you access and use as part of your work on emerging themes.

In particular you need to know the source.

- **Who**? Who has produced the information? What are their credentials or area of expertise?
- **Why**? What are their motives for producing it – is there a bias in their view of the topic?
- **When**? How old is the information? In today's fast moving markets things date very quickly, so take care with dates.
- **How**? How was the information collected? If it is from research how big were the sample sizes and how were they selected?

Since there may be limitations in the quality of any one source of information you need to consider several different sources. The more the same '*story*' emerges from a wide variety of sources, the more confidence you can have. **And don't be afraid to be critical**. At this level of the profession it is important that you challenge and question. At one level that means questioning your information sources. At another, more strategic, level you might question how useful the rational approach to strategy development and market analysis is. In such rapidly changing markets, is a model like Porter's Five Forces a help or a hindrance? Emergent rather than planned approaches may be more valuable in today's turbulent markets.

Take time to review two resources recommended by the examiner.

Porter, M (2008) *"The five competitive forces that shape strategy".* Harvard Business Review, Jan Vol 86 (1) pp 78-93. Ebsco link via CIM site.

Bowman, C (2008) *"Generic strategies: A substitute for thinking? 360°"* The Ashridge Journal. Spring pp 6-11. ∎

4.3 The potential impact on marketing practice

In this chapter you have seen two examples where, if you follow the theme through, you can see the potential impact on marketing strategies, activities and tactics.

In the case of children's health, changing attitudes to advertising and product development for children's markets is likely. Changes may be voluntary or enforced by legislation. Note that such changes will impact not just on the media companies selling advertising space.

In the case of the older consumer there are a number of changes likely to emerge.

(a) Marketers will stop treating over 50s together as one big demographic segment. Segmentation of this 50% of the population may be based on more detailed or relevant criteria such as activity level, health and degree of independence rather than age.

The following diagram outlines possible dimensions to segment this market.

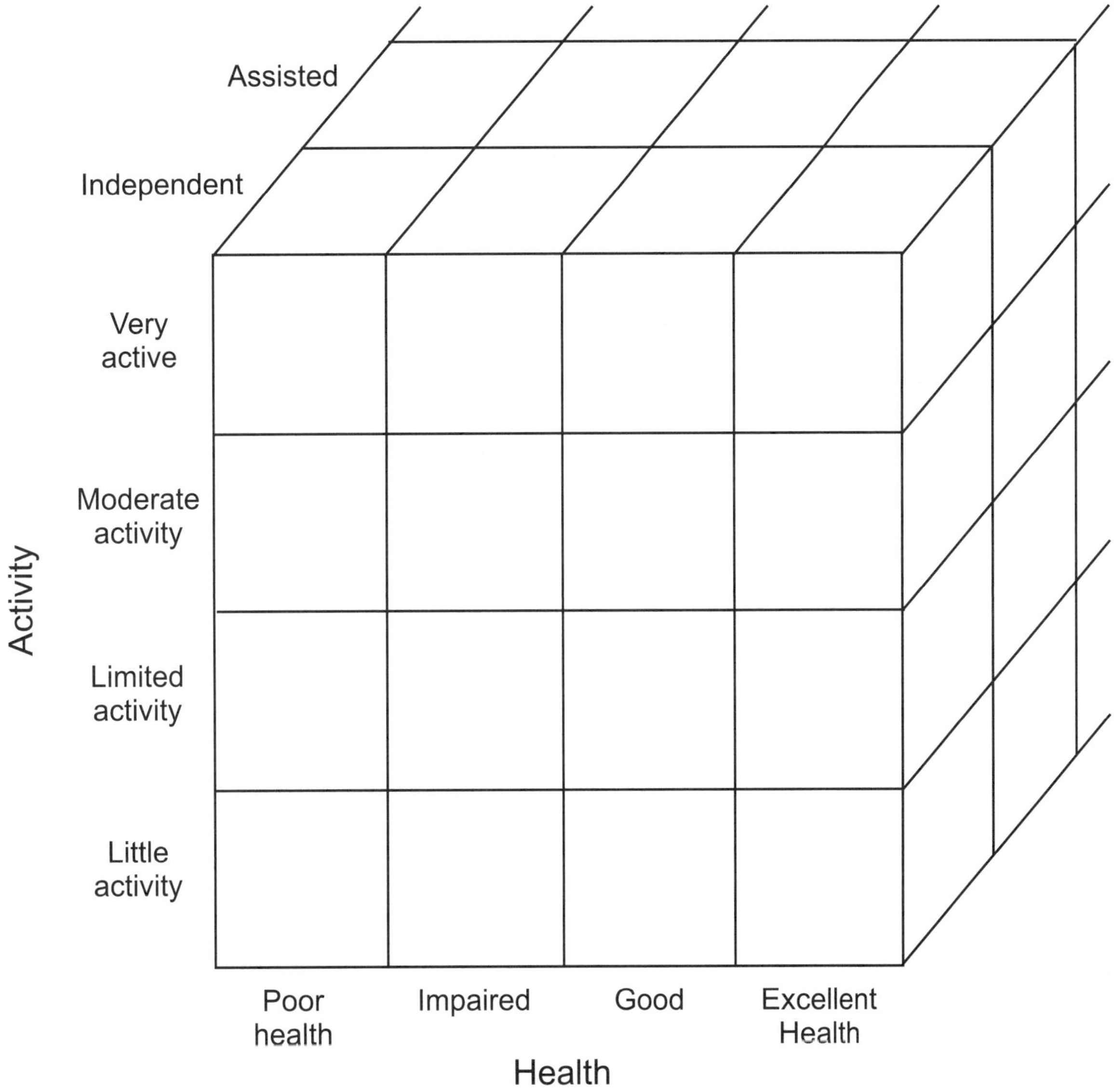

[Diagram: A 3D cube showing market segmentation dimensions. The vertical axis is "Activity" with levels: Little activity, Limited activity, Moderate activity, Very active. The horizontal axis is "Health" with levels: Poor health, Impaired, Good, Excellent Health. The depth axis shows: Independent, Assisted.]

If you consider your market of over 50s as a Rubic cube (as shown above) and start thinking about dimensions likely to drive their behaviour and needs as a customer, you begin to see the range of 'segments' there could potentially be.

At a more tactical level aspects of accessibility have already been addressed by legislation. This could be expanded with motorised shopping trolleys in stores and 'smart' products able to read out instructions to the user.

The faster organisations recognise the financial value of this group, the more innovative solutions to meet their needs will be. The success of console games like the Brain Trainer demonstrate the financial value locked up in a '*laggard*' segment of the market.

4.4 The need for innovation

The examiners will be looking for you to demonstrate innovation and creativity in your advice on how a sector should respond to the identified emerging theme. You will need to assess what is already happening, and also to push that to the next level and think about how marketers might change marketing activity, use new approaches or methods in response to a change in the market.

ACTIVITY 6

 application

As a final activity in this Chapter give yourself one hour to build up your own sector specific resources and information sources list.

Try to get examples for all the sources identified earlier. Talk to colleagues, visit the CIM website and the sites for sector associations and industry trade bodies.

Learning objective review

Learning objectives	Covered
1 Map how a range of changes may bring about emerging themes	☑ Used mind maps to see interlinked forces. ☑ Adapted 'circles' from total product concept to consider how changes at different levels could be viewed. ☑ Used childhood obesity and older customers as examples.
2 Be able to use Kurt Lewin's force field analysis to help assess the strength of changes and help evaluate which should be acted upon.	☑ Used both force field and Porter's Five Forces as models to help assess the strength of an emerging trend. ☑ Considered how relevant rational approaches are in rapidly changing market conditions.
3 'Forecast' how macro level changes might impact different sectors	☑ Considered how the same theme would impact a number of different sectors.
4 Use a **variety** of sources.	☑ Identified a range of sources. ☑ Considered the factors you need to assess before using your sources. ☑ Started a checklist of information sources relevant to your sector.

Quick quiz

1   Is it important to be able to map the sequence of inter-related changes in the environment?

2   Should the marketing professional treat all emerging themes equally?

3   How might Force Field Analysis help you assess an emerging theme?

4   On a Force Field map what would different thickness of arrows indicate?

5   What is a restraining force in Force Field Analysis?

6   Why is Porter's Five Forces model useful in your analysis?

7   What sources of information may be available to support your analysis?

1 **The case of the older consumer**

You may well have included different factors on your mind map but you will have the same sort of factors all driving an ageing but economically and socially more active customer set.

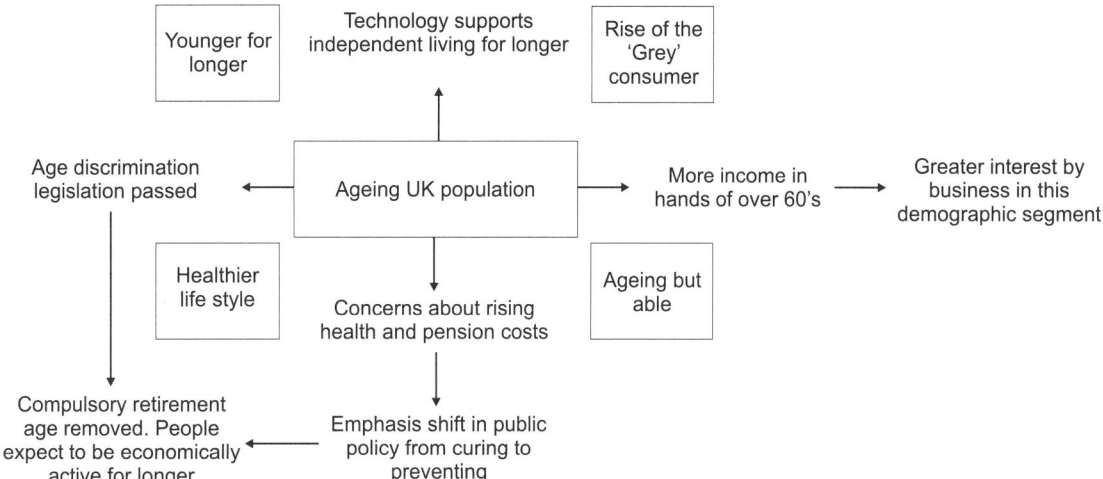

2 Again there is no single answer so you may have thought of different factors.

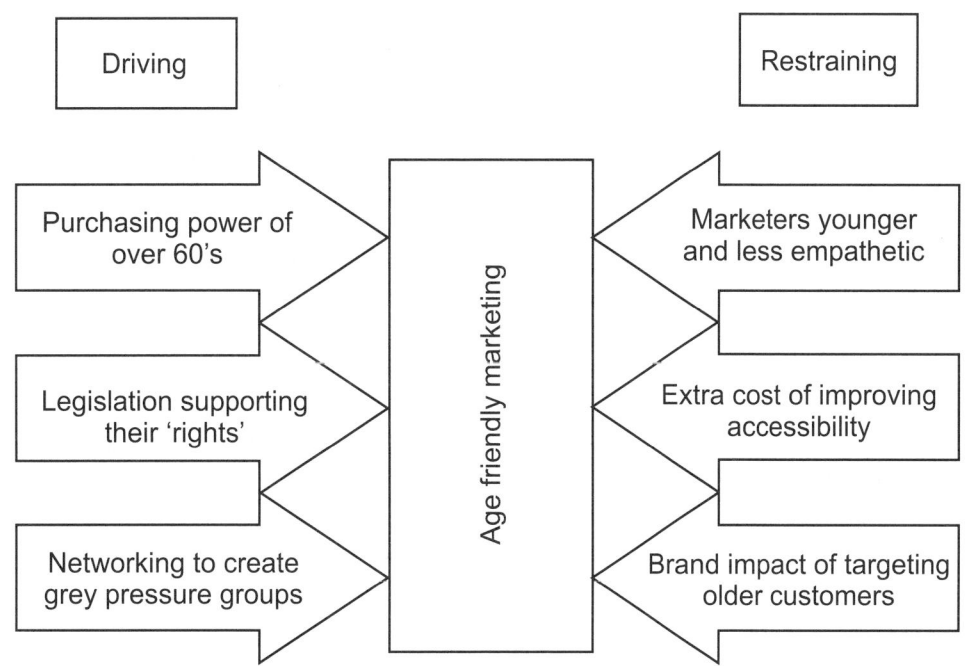

3   We are thinking about the future so there are no certain answers. The ideas and observations below will give you some ideas to compare with your own answers.

Sector/ Industry	Implications and industry level issues or responses
NHS	Growing numbers of older patients will require new approaches to rehabilitation after falls, illnesses etc. *'Quality of life'* prioritisation criteria may be needed to help decide between competing services that could be developed/ delivered. Public debate about priorities leads to individuals having greater control of their own personal budget for the health and social care providers marketing directly to individual service users.
Insurance	Costs and prices of a range of policies will rise if people live longer, for example private health insurance. Competing firms will find ways of '*including*' older customers. For example lower motor insurance premiums for careful drivers. New types of products to '*insure*' for extra support in the home. A public sector under pressure from increased demand may not deliver service levels required, thus encouraging people to be prepared to '*top-up*' from private insurance.
Grocery retail	The older consumer will be a key segment and the big stores will compete to be the most '*age friendly*'. Delivery services, wider aisles and trolleys that aid mobility may be amongst the changes you could expect. In turn the grocery retailers will demand from their suppliers: • Easy open packaging • Option of smaller/simple portion packs and sizes • Larger writing and labelling to help those with poorer sight
Leisure services	A growing market likely to be rich in both time and income. New leisure time activities and options may be expected to emerge. In the 1980's and 90's this segment was the catalyst for the re-emergence of the cruise lines. This group wants activity, new forms of social club and easier access for concerts and sporting events may be anticipated. There is a big opportunity here for digital solutions. Social networks for an increasingly IT savvy group and virtual concepts, online games and gaming are all likely to appeal to this market.
Manufacturers of consumer durables	Easy to use and appropriate for smaller households will be key requirements for durables.
House builders	Already future proofing for an older population is underway with, for example, wider doorways to allow wheel chair access. Other issues may include: • Designs that ensure easy access to all living areas • The integration of smart technologies that will for example monitor bath water temperatures and ensure doors and windows are secure. • Power points at easy to reach heights etc.
Your own sector	Your answer here will be specific to your sector

4   **Health care provision for the over 60s**

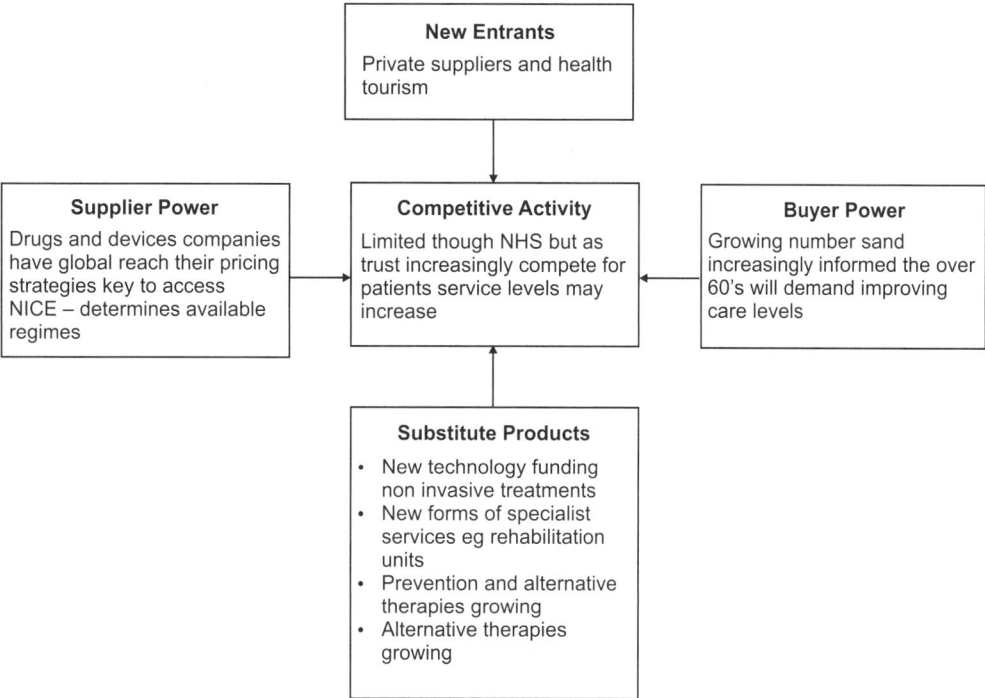

Conclusions:

(a) Increasing pressure on the NHS and units within the NHS to find innovative solutions and service improvements for NHS.

(b) There are some powerful suppliers to the NHS and supply chain management and procurement will be critical to future efficiency levels. Therefore potentially there will be increasing restrictions on pharmaceutical and devices companies marketing directly to medical professionals. NICE and procurement teams may limit choices and mean marketing in this sector needs re-thinking.

(c) Competitive activity is likely to increase, caused by the market created within the NHS and also new suppliers. These include private sector suppliers taking on NHS contracts to deliver services as well as private hospitals (at home and abroad) offering alternative care packages. There will also be competition in the form of alternative therapies and technology breakthroughs.

Over time over 60s patients may be attractive targets for the NHS and its competition. They will represent a flow of funding and source of additional income. You are likely to have variations in your response depending on how much you know about the health sector.

5   **Identifying sources**

Your list might have included any of the following:

– Academic journals
– Practitioner publications
– Trade association/sector reports
– Government reports and strategies
– Private reports and data
– Websites
– Newspapers and magazines
– User groups, forums, blogs
– Observation, industry level mystery shopping

6   **Your own research**

Quiz answers

1. Not necessarily, it is more important for you to see the range of factors coming together. Different sectors may become aware of an emerging theme for different reasons and from a different perspective.

2. No, not all emerging themes will be equally significant or indeed as long lasting as others. Some sectors will be impacted severely, and others will not.

3. It provides a model for taking account of all the factors drawing a theme and those working against it. In this way you may get more insight into how 'serious' or 'real' an emerging theme may become!

4. The thickness of arrows can be used to indicate the seriousness or extent of the force.

5. A force working against the emerging theme. So if people are forecast to live longer in future generations the ill health and lack of fitness of today's children may be a restraining force.

6. Porter's Five Forces model encourages you to look at the changes at marketing level.

7. Academic journals, trade and government statistics, newspapers, websites, blogs, observation.

References

Lewin K. (1943)."*Defining the Field at a Given Time*." Psychological Review. 50: 292-310. Republished in *Resolving Social Conflicts & Field Theory in Social Science,* Washington, D.C.: American Psychological Association, 1997.

Office of National Statistics (2009) "*Population Estimates*" Available online at: http://www.statistics.gov.uk/cci/nugget.asp?ID=6 [accessed 12th June 2009].

Porter, M (2008) The five competitive forces that shape strategy. Harvard Business Review, Jan Vol 86 (1) pp 78-93.

Chapter 4
Emerging themes in organisations' environment

Topic list

1. Politics and the law
2. Contemporary economic opportunities and challenges
3. Demographic change
4. Social and cultural change
5. Technological change
6. The environment

Introduction

This chapter is intended to give you an introduction to some of the key changes and emerging themes at macro level. As you have already seen, not all changes impact on all sectors or do so in the same way or to the same extent. The coverage of macro trends cannot be exhaustive but we have examined one or two trends and changes in each of the core macro environmental areas.

ASSIGNMENT TIP

evaluation

When you are visiting sites to follow up on topics under review take the opportunity to check out links and content that may be specifically relevant to your sector or customer base.

By its very nature the syllabus and focus for this module are always evolving so the content which follows should be treated as indicative only – you will need to add to it information on the most current developments for your own sector.

Syllabus linked learning objectives

By the end of the chapter you will be able to evaluate critically the impact of the emerging themes listed below in the context of a specific sector or industry:

Learning objectives	Syllabus link
1 Changes in political governance systems and political focus	1.1
2 Contemporary economic opportunities and challenges	1.1, 1.2
3 Demographic changes	1.1, 1.2
4 Social change at local and global levels	1.1, 1.2
5 Emerging technologies	1.1, 1.2
6 Environmental challenges	1.1, 1.2

1 Politics and the law

You might like to create your own '*maps*' of the key themes emerging from each of these areas – we have started one for politics and the law.

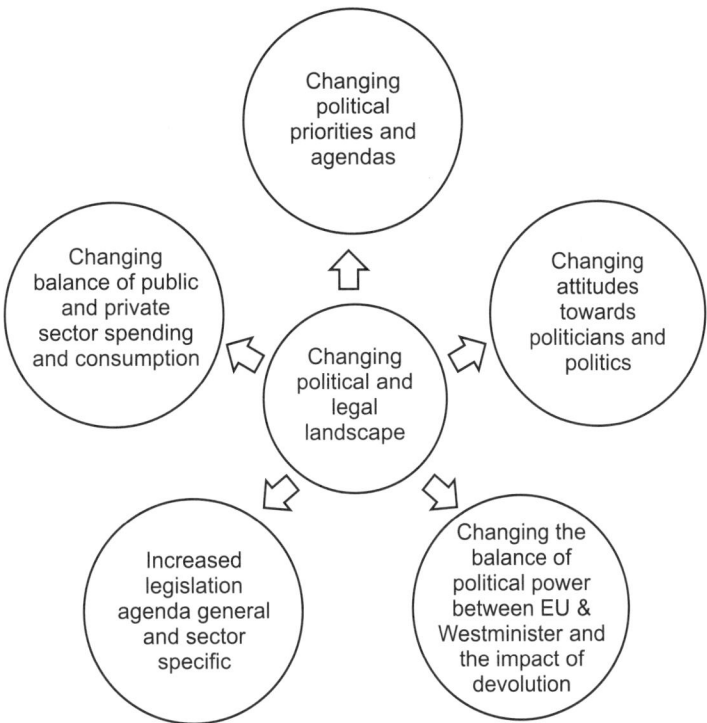

1.1 Changing attitudes

In 2009, the Daily Telegraph in the UK revealed the extent of the abuse of the expenses and allowances system operated for UK politicians. As a theme, its emergence could have been observed by an alert MP or even party. There has been debate and discussion about the system for several years. Details have been requested under the Freedom of Information Act and there have been a steady stream of proposals for change that in the main were rejected. A major opportunity was missed. Had one of the parties forecast the appetite for greater transparency, it could perhaps have taken steps to ensure its MPs were acting in the spirit as well as the letter of the rules.

In the end all parties seem to have been as culpable as each other in the way they used the system.

Taken on top of revelations about pay and bonuses in the financial sector, the stage has been set for a push towards greater public access to information on remuneration policies and strategies. It could become another force pushing the devolution agenda with people demanding greater control and transparency over public expenditure, particularly in the light of the harsh public sector spending cuts that have been flagged as being necessary by the new UK government in 2010. It has without doubt added to the sense of public cynicism which in turn will influence broad consumer attitudes.

 ACTIVITY 1   *evaluation*

Take a few minutes to consider how the issue of politicians' pay is being played out today. Has it escalated and is starting to become an emerging theme or has it faded into yesterday's news?

If you are studying in a non-UK centre, consider similar themes within your current country of residence.

1.2 Changing political climate

Whilst events like the one above can clearly change attitudes, political climates change with change in political leadership. Around the world there are regular changes in leadership in many countries. With those changes come new attitudes to international trade and relations, economic policy and local legislation. As a marketer working in the global market place you need to keep checking for changes in political climate.

How for example might these political changes influence business in the coming years?

November 2008 Barack Obama becomes America's first African American President

Obama campaigned as a technocratic agent of change and not a path breaking civil rights figure, but already the difference in political attitude is clear – greater international empathy and awareness of other views and cultures will surely make a difference on the international stage.

May 2009 Jacob Zuma sworn in as President of South Africa

A man of the people throughout his political career, Mr Zuma, popularly known as "JZ", has honed his image as a champion of the poor and oppressed. He enjoys strong support among trade unionists and the communist party - an ANC ally - as it is believed he will redistribute South Africa's wealth in favour of the poor.

Spring 2010 UK General Election

The Conservative / Liberal Democrat coalition government that came to power in May 2010 has already warned of a 'painful' period of spending cuts to bring the UK's deficit under control. What will this mean for those with public sector customers?

1.3 Devolution changes political landscape

 KEY CONCEPT  concept

Devolution is the statutory granting of powers from the central government of a state to government at a subnational level, such as a regional, local, or state level. It differs from federalism in that the powers devolved may be temporary and ultimately reside in central government, thus the state remains, de jure, unitary.

Any devolved parliaments or assemblies can be repealed by central government in the same way an ordinary statute can be. Federal systems, or federacies, differ in that state or provincial government is guaranteed in the constitution. Australia, Canada and the United States have federal systems, and have constitutions (as do some of their constituent states or provinces). They also have Territories, with less power and authority than a state or province.

The devolution can be mainly financial, e.g. giving areas a budget which was formerly administered by central government. However, the power to make legislation relevant to the area may also be granted.

One of the emerging themes highlighted by the Senior Examiner is the question of devolution.

Key Points about Devolution in the UK

- Devolution has been relatively successful and popular in Wales and Scotland. The English seem content with continued, centralised government from Westminster and have not been persuaded of the benefits of regional government (with the exception of the GLA in London where a similar model of regional government is now well-established currently under the leadership of Boris Johnson). There is a significant basis of support for devolution among citizens in both Protestant and Catholic communities in Northern Ireland – including Sinn Fein and DUP voters – though political elites there have shown little inclination as yet to respond to that support and make devolution work. The government has however continued to decentralise administrative functions to appointed bodies in the regions. The growth of '*administrative governance*' has brought with it as yet unresolved problems of accountability, duplication and inefficiency. This is because de-centralisation of buying in this way technically reduces buyer power making it easier for suppliers to regional bodies and government to negotiate better deals.

- According to the UK's Economic and Social Research Council, ESCR, there is little evidence to suggest that an '*economic dividend*' should be expected from devolution, or has yet appeared. Devolution – even administrative devolution in England – appears to lead to a widening of regional economic disparities. The UK government only has limited abillity to intervene to secure UK wide economic balance.

- For companies trying to operate at a national level devolution can make sales and marketing more difficult with variations in purchasing behaviours and protocols at regional level.

- According to the work on devolution done by ESRC there has been surprisingly little conflict between the devolved administrations and central government and Westminster so far. There has been innovation and divergence of priorities and actions but little sharing and '*learning*' across the authorities.

- The main reasons for this period of calm were temporary:
    - Labour's role as the leading partner in government in Westminster, Scotland and Wales;
    - A general growth in public expenditure which has limited distributional conflicts.

    The election of a Conservative / Liberal Democrat coalition in May 2010 and the clamp down on public spending which will have to come over the next few years is likely to cause many more disputes and mechanisms to handle these will be key.

  ACTIVITY 2  evaluation

1 Do your own research into devolution. Visit www.parliament.uk and read their paper – Introduction to Devolution

2 Visit the ESRC web site at www.ESRC.com

3 The Devolution and Constitutional Change Programme was set up by ESRC in 2000 to explore the series of devolution reforms which have established new political institutions in Scotland, Wales, Northern Ireland, London and the other English regions since 1997.

   35 research projects have been selected to pull together a critical mass of researchers from across the social sciences to dissect the implications of devolution for the UK state, society and economy.

4 The Smith Institute, published a paper 'Double Devolution' about the reform of local government.

Find out more about possible sources.

About the Smith Institute	About ERSC
The Smith Institute was founded in the memory of the late Rt Hon John Smith. It is an independent think tank that undertakes research, education and events. They provide a platform for national and international discussion on a wide range of public policy issues concerning social justice, community, governance, enterprise, economy, trade, and the environment.	The Economic and Social Research Council (ESRC) funds research and training in social and economic issues. It is an independent organisation, established by Royal Charter, but receives most of its funding through the Department for Innovation, Universities and Skills. Its planned expenditure for 2008/09 is £203 million, which funds over 2,500 researchers in academic institutions and policy research institutes throughout the UK. It also supports more than 2,000 postgraduate students. ESRC began in 1965 as the Social Science Research Council, comprising social science committees covering 14 disciplines ranging from anthropology to statistics. In 1983 the council was restructured under the new name of Economic and Social Research Council, focusing on six research areas: economic affairs, education and human development, environment and planning, government and law, industry and employment, and social affairs.

1.4 The implications of changing political attitudes, climate or systems

The implications of big changes like devolution are felt at sector level. Decentralisation of decision-making becomes a theme which is reflected across health, education and other public service areas. Each of these changes will impact on organisations trying to provide services and support to public sector customers.

At a local level changes in political attitudes can impact on local government decisions including planning decisions. How green belt is used, permission for road improvement schemes negotiated and new developments approved impact the on many different sectors.

You may be interested in looking at a 2006 paper from Friends of the Earth which takes a critical view of how supermarkets in the UK are allowed to influence local planning decisions.

www.foe.co.uk/resource/briefings/callingtheshots.pdf

1.5 The legal environment

The political climate will influence the priorities around new legislation but they are separate dimensions of the PEST environment. It is also important to remember that legislative changes can be generated at EU as well as Westminster level so a good environmental observer will be watching for emerging themes in the broader European context.

  application

Legal changes that have had an impact

Take a few minutes to think about legal changes that have had an impact on specific sectors, consumer behaviour or marketing activity recently. Try to identify five examples from your own sector or broader business.

Your list will inevitably be different from ours but you can make the comparison at the end of the Chapter.

 MARKETING AT WORK application

The Olympics 2012 will without doubt attract a lot of interest and will generate opportunities across many sectors from construction to hospitality, tourism to sports management. Some estimates claim the Games will deliver a £2 billion bonus for the British economy through extra visitors from abroad.

Some believe that the regulations and legislation surrounding the use of the Olympics in marketing activity will restrict business but it doesn't seem like it is deterring many. According to The CIM Marketing Trends Survey Autumn 2007, 41% of working marketers say that it is likely their organisation will undertake some marketing activities connected to the London 2012 Games. This figure rises among those organisations with more than £100 million turnover and is also higher in the south of the country.

You can find out more about how the Olympics legislation may impact on marketing activities for the Olympics by doing some more research. Some of the sources you might look up include:

Google the London Olympic Games and Paralympic Games Act 2006

Article in The Independent, 5 May 2006: London Olympics team sets sights on sponsorship gold

Article in The Times, 5 November 2005: 2012 Games sponsors sold on logo no-go areas

Brand Guides by London 2012: Understand how the laws protecting the London 2012 brand apply to your business

Marketing the Olympics factfile, CIM

The Olympics: getting it right (www.cim.co.uk/resources/emergingthemes)

And why do the Olympics matter? Well consider the extract below from the Guardian 18th August 2008.

 MARKETING AT WORK  application

The real Olympics competition: Nike and Adidas claim China's heroes

Global sportswear firms battle it out for a multi-billion dollar prize

Never mind the athletics. The real battle in Beijing is not the struggle to top the medal table, but the multi-billion dollar fight between two giant brands intent on conquering the fastest growing sportswear market in the world. Adidas and Nike have invested unprecedented sums in wooing Chinese consumers during the Olympics. The German firm is estimated to have spent $190m (£100m) on sponsorship and associated marketing; its US rival has stumped up close to $150m.

That is a lot of marketing budget so it is not surprising that legislation is needed to ensure sponsors get an opportunity which is clearly differentiated from the marketing activity of non-sponsors. Magic formula icons are: format, concept, application or evaluation.

1.6 Marketing and the law

Legal issues have a direct influence on how we as marketers do our job. According to CIM's Hot Topic Paper **No Marketer is an Island: Marketing and the Law** there is no doubt that marketers face increasingly restrictive legislation. Heavy-handed bills are regularly placed before governments in the UK, the US and further afield. Marketers face confusion over the number of laws, regulations and codes that they have to know about. Increasingly, marketers even need to know about laws that have been passed elsewhere in the world.

The days of laissez-faire marketing are long gone. We must work out how to market our products and services fairly and effectively. Since ignorance of the law is no defence, marketing teams need to be proactive in self-regulation in order to avoid brand damage and costly legal proceedings should they make a mistake.

 ACTIVITY 4 evaluation

Visit the CIM website and read their papers:

No Marketer is an Island: Marketing and the Law which considers how best to tackle such legal compliance.

The **Long Arm of the Law: Marketers and Legislation** asks marketers to question what they know, consider whether their legal compliance is all it should be - and think hard about the implications for the future.

2 Contemporary economic opportunities and challenges

2.1 An economic overview

The following overview of the key economic changes is a little light on opportunities. The near collapse of the international banking system and subsequent credit crunch is going to create long term challenges that will impact every sector of the economy.

In the public sector it is inevitable that purse strings will have to tighten as the UK Government works to rebalance the books.

The following diagram summarises some of the likely changes.

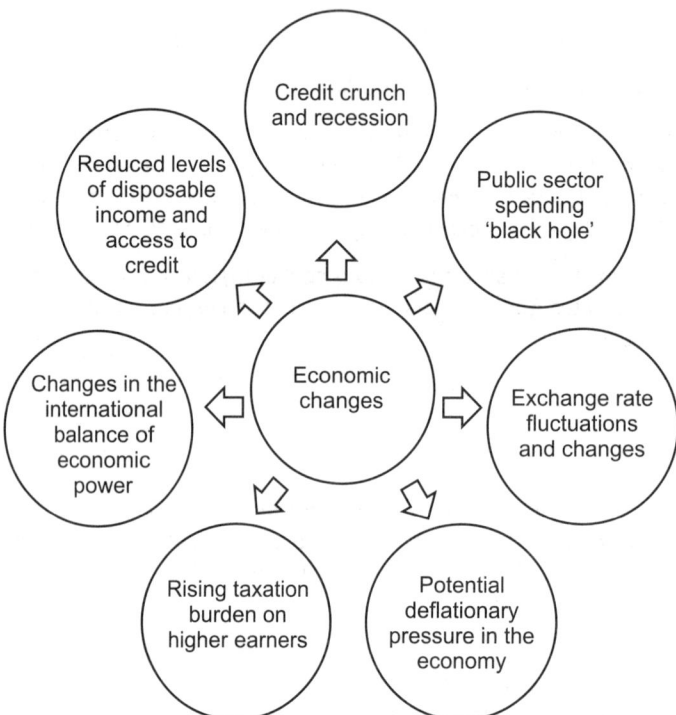

This is not just a localised challenge. Across the globe governments are addressing the fall out from the near collapse of the banking system. Some countries have already come off badly, for example Iceland. Others like China and India will have their rapid growth rates slowed but are likely to end up as the engines of growth to pull the world out of the recession.

The economic environment is particularly important in forecasting future activity levels because demand has to be backed by the ability to pay for it to be relevant. Changes in that ability to pay are caused by:

- Changes in the level of economic activity determined by the level of employment and productivity
- Changes in the size of the population affecting average incomes
- Changes in inflation impacting on the purchasing value of income nationally
- Changes in exchange rates impacting on purchase values between countries
- Changes in tax policy and the tax burden influencing the balance of public and private sector expenditure and the distribution of income
- Changes in the availability of, or social attitude to, credit and savings which impact on the marginal propensity to spend or save.

All of these changes will alter the economic health of customers, be they business or household customers and so the marketing professional needs to be able to understand how they impact on their customers. There are plenty of statistics available to help which will provide regional insights as well as national ones.

2.1.1 Example

The Office for National Statistics (ONS) is the executive office of the UK Statistics Authority, a non-ministerial department which reports directly to Parliament. ONS is the UK Government's single largest statistical producer. The National Statistician is also the UK Statistics Authority's Chief Executive and principal statistical adviser.

In 2008/09 total ONS budget was £237 million. The organisation employs some 3,900 staff (of whom 1,300 are field staff who collect information for social surveys).

A visit to its website will provide you information about the 2011 census – which is being implemented under a new brand.

Note: In most European countries you will find the National Statistics Institute performs similar functions at country level.

  ACTIVITY 5   evaluation

Visit National Statistics Online *'UK Snapshot'* to get an up to date picture of the current state of the economy. Remember that even if your target market are other companies (eg B2B) their demand will be influenced by end-user demand – in other words theirs is derived demand, so forecasts of consumer changes will provide you with insights about emerging themes which may impact on your business later.

Have a look around the site to familiarise yourself with the sort of data that is available.

2.2 The recession and its impact

The important thing about emerging themes, as you have already seen, is how changes at the macro level impact on how markets behave and influence customer needs and behaviours.

The credit crunch/recession has already been featured in examples earlier in this text. It has caught the headlines for a number of reasons:

- The speed of events
- The global nature of those events
- The wide impact of problems in the core financial sector
- The seriousness of the legacy of events and the actions taken to deal with them both nationally and internationally.

There is no shortage of information about the causes of the crash, nor a shortage of forecasts about its long term shape and severity. This is a good example of how it will be important to take in a number of sources when trying to assess the severity and implications of change.

  ACTIVITY 6   application

Take a lighter look at the causes of the financial problems and the sub-prime market by looking at Bird and Fortune's view of the credit crunch.

http://uk.youtube.com/watch?v=hXBcmqwTV9s

2.3 Recession at sector level

There is no doubt that the recession has impacted on some sectors more seriously than others. The global car industry and construction have been hard hit but also have benefited from direct government support to try to help them.

To date those whose main customers have been the Public Sector, for example the pharmaceuticals industry, have been relatively unaffected, but, as we have indicated, cuts in public sector finance have to follow.

  ACTIVITY 7 application

You need to do some research to find sources of information that can help you evaluate the credit crunch and global recession (in the context of your own sector and industry). Spread your research net wide and include the media, BBC and newspapers as well as YouTube and of course your own trade association and industry bodies. Try talking to colleagues and do your own jury forecasting.

2.4 Changes for marketing

2.4.1 A more strategic role for marketing

Within sectors the pain of recession has not been felt equally. However as your saw in Chapter 1, recession forces the pace of change to become a '*buyer's market*'. With less active customers in the market and less disposable income, competition to win custom intensifies.

Strategic marketing activity has accordingly started to move centre stage. There is evidence that the need to be customer focused and really understand customer needs and deliver solutions they value has been accepted. This change altering the role of marketing within organisations is still an emerging theme, but one that marketers have been arguing for and one you need to monitor within your sector and organisation. Certainly the most forward looking organisations do not appear to be using the recession as a reason to slash marketing activity, though they may be reappraising it.

 ACTIVITY 8 evaluation

Recession Hits Retail in South Africa

Take a look at the questions below and compare your answers with the feedback at the end of the chapter.

S. AFRICA: Recession Fears Loom As Retail Sales Drop In March

South Africa may have become the latest country to have slipped into a recession, after latest figures revealed lower consumer spending, and weak manufacturing and mining output. In March, retail sales in the country were down 5.3% year-on-year, the sharpest fall since at least 2003 according to a revised deflator introduced this year. This followed a revised drop in sales of 4.4% in February. For the first quarter, retail sales were down 2.9% year-on-year.

Retailers have been hit by the sluggish economy, with consumer spending down after the central bank raised interest rates by a cumulative 5 percentage points between June 2006 and June 2008. Although interest rates started coming down in December, households are still weighed down by high debt levels. This led to the economy contracting by 1.8% in the fourth quarter of 2008, the first such decline in a decade. (Source: Namnews - Thursday 14th May 2009)

If you were a marketing consultant advising South Africa's retail sector what advice would you give them about:

(a) Prioritising customers?
(b) How to segment their market to take account of the impact of recession?
(c) The tactical marketing approaches and activities they should use?
(d) If marketing budgets have to be cut where to look for savings?

Emerging Themes

The longer lasting changes in marketing behaviour may involve a speedier adoption of new media opportunities for communication (with a knock-on impact on advertising incomes) and greater innovation in segmentation and developing customer solutions.

2.4.2 Changes in customer behaviour

The emerging themes that we cannot yet be sure about are those that will impact on longer term customer behaviour. They could include the rise of the careful customer, the increased propensity for shopping around, negotiating deals and accepting non-branded alternatives. These changes will make it more challenging to establish and build long term customer relationships and an increase in transactional behaviour will have a negative impact on return on marketing investment.

In business to business sectors the pressure on budgets is likely to intensify and encourage the professionalisation of buying through procurement managers, tendering processes and so on. Again these developments would not make the marketers' job easier but would make it difficult to build relationships with customers and users and add to the cost of the sales process.

www.foe.co.uk/resource/briefings/callingtheshots.pdf

2.5 Network governance

 KEY CONCEPT concept

Network governance is interfirm coordination, characterised by organic or informal systems, in contrast to bureaucratic structures within firms and formal contractual relationships between them.

Another of the emerging themes highlighted by the Senior Examiner is the question of network governance.

As a concept, network governance encourages increased efficiency for organisations existing in highly turbulent environments, by co-ordinating internal teams with external partners (such as those in a supply chain) and encouraging permanent communication at all the various management levels.

Any given firm in a supply chain has its own relationships and connections with multiple other players: multiple suppliers and customers, industry contacts, partners/collaborators and advisers – any or all of whom may themselves be connected with each other.

Network relationships

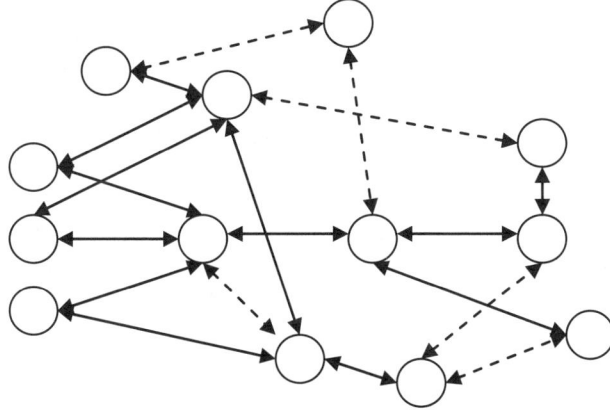

The network metaphor is arguably a more realistic model for mapping and analysing business relationships.

- It raises the possibility of a **wider range of connections and collaborations** in the future (eg knowledge sharing, alliances and co-promotions) which may offer mutual advantages – and help to add value for the customer.

- It also recognises the potential of what has been called the **'extended enterprise'**: extending the capability of a firm by tapping into the resources and competences of other network contributors (for example, by outsourcing activities like call centres to partners better equipped to undertake them). Some of this extended enterprise, these days, may well be 'virtual': that is, connected purely by Information & Communication Technology links, such as the Internet.

Long-term, mutually-beneficial relationships with a customer, competitor or other stakeholder may be developed using a number of approaches now and in the future:

Relationship	Comments
Partnerships	Close, collaborative, mutually beneficial long-term relationships, usually with other members of the business system or **supply chain**: eg suppliers or service providers, distributors, retailers and (in B2B markets) customers. Partnership relations focus on **aligning the objectives** of both parties, and allowing both to **share in the value gains** created by the collaboration. The relationship between a client and a long-term advertising agency, business consultancy or major supplier will often be classed as partnerships, for example.
Strategic alliances	Formally structured relationships, in which two companies legally contract to cooperate in limited, specified ways (eg collaborative promotions or product cross-selling) to achieve specific commercial objectives that are of benefit to both parties. One example is the various promotional alliances between credit card companies and airlines, to offer joint loyalty incentives.
Joint ventures	Formal arrangements whereby two independent companies establish a new company which they jointly own and manage. Their other businesses remain separate from this new, shared venture. (Where more than two companies enter the arrangement, it is called a '**consortium**'.) Joint ventures are often used to overcome barriers to entry into international markets: Western companies operating in Eastern Europe and China, for example, have often been required to form joint ventures with local partners. One provides technical and managerial expertise and investment, while the other supplies access to labour and local markets.
Networks	Looser, dynamic, more informal affiliations of autonomous and broadly equal organisations, which exchange information and pursue ongoing (typically long-term) relationships for mutual benefit. Rather than direct contractual or financial obligations, the relationships are held together by collaboration, communication, trust and mutual advantage.
Virtual organisations	A special form of network, where companies (or units of a single company) collaborate, co-ordinate their activities and share data using **information communications technology (ICT)** as their main – or only – point of contact. Relationships may also be formed in **virtual communities** (customer-to-customer or C2C networks), such as online clubs, You Tube or Face-Book, for example, which support user networking and content sharing.
E-relationships	Relationships, networks and interaction based on information and communication technology (ICT): email, websites, e-commerce, e-procurement, e-learning, e-publishing, Internet banking, virtual team-working, virtual communities and so on.
Customisation	Relationship ties developed through the adaptation of processes, products, services and messages to the specific requirements of an individual customer or other party: a form of 'one-to-one' marketing. Customisation may be a way of adding **unique value** through a relationship: Dell Computers, for example, allows individual customers to configure their own hardware and software requirements. It may also represent **integration and mutual dependency** (eg a supplier developing equipment or systems specifically for a major customer), which ties the parties together.
Internal customer relationships	Relationships between functions, units and levels in an organisation. Organisations comprise internal supply chains, communication networks and markets. Each link in the value chain towards the end consumer can be seen as the 'customer' of the one before it: service must be delivered, and value added, particularly in cross-functional relationships, in order to co-ordinate the activities of the firm towards customer value.

MARKETING AT WORK

Kodak's Criteria for Evaluating Supplier Partnerships

- Amount of technical support
- Number of innovative ideas
- Supplier's ability to communicate effectively on important issues
- Flexibility shown by the supplier
- Cycle time, responsiveness and improvement shown
- Identification with Kodak goals: are our goals common?
- Level of trust that exists in dealing with the supplier
- Strength of the relationship at each plant

2.5.1 Collaborative supplier partnerships

In a collaborative approach, the buyer seeks to develop longer-term relationships with a smaller number of preferred suppliers. The strategic view is that both organisations can benefit from seeking ways of adding value in the supply chain, to the ultimate benefit of the end consumer. Relationship management is based on trust, mutual obligation and benefit (rather than compliance with contract terms), and information sharing. The supplier participates with the buyer in looking for improvements and innovations: they jointly set targets for improvements in cost and quality, and meet regularly to discuss progress towards achieving these targets. Information is shared more or less freely (in areas of shared activity) in both directions, in order to support joint problem-solving and development.

Collaboration can be seen on a spectrum. At the tactical end, suppliers may be invited to participate in new product development projects, quality drives or cost-reduction programmes, say. At the high-trust, high-integration end of the spectrum are:

- **Outsourcing relationships**: a supplier carries out part of the firm's activities (eg production, data processing or telesales) on its behalf, under contract

- **Strategic alliances**: contractual collaboration in particular areas (eg co-branding or joint entry into a new international market)

- **Partnership relationships**: buyers and suppliers agree to collaborate closely over the long term, sharing information and ideas for development.

The **benefits of collaborative supplier relationships** can be summarised as follows.

Benefits to the supplier	Benefits to the buyer
There will be established points of contact, enabling the development of trust	Purchasing attention is focused on developing deeper relationships with fewer suppliers
Better information about the buyer and its needs enables the supplier to manage the buyer's expectations and offer better service	Better information, supplier commitment and collaborative improvement-seeking should result in better service and quality gains
Better information (and/or systems integration) allows forward planning	A smaller supplier base and systems integration lead to process efficiencies and reduced sourcing costs
Joint improvement, development and value gains will be shared by the supplier	The buyer may get preferential treatment (eg in the case of supply shortages or emergency orders) arising from goodwill
The supplier is likely to get more business, as preferred supplier	The buyer should be able to develop a high degree of trust and confidence in the supplier

Collaborative strategies are currently fashionable, but it is important to note that a collaborative approach is not necessarily the 'best' approach to supply chain relations in all circumstances. Co-operative or partnership relations take time and effort to develop, and may not be worth the investment for the purchase of routine items – especially since the buyer will also be missing out on opportunities to drive price down by adversarial bargaining.

There are also drawbacks, risks and obstacles in getting close or 'cosy' with suppliers, or in getting 'locked in' to long-term supply contracts. There is the risk of being locked into a relationship with the 'wrong' partners (incompatible – or unethical, which brings additional reputational risk from being associated with them). There is risk in exchanging information, possibly losing control over confidential data and intellectual property. Over-dependence on a small group of suppliers may make the buyer vulnerable to supply risk if they fail or suffer disruption. Long-term supply partners may get complacent and cease to give excellent service or prices. And high switching costs may be a constraint if better alternative suppliers emerge in the market.

 ACTIVITY 9 Application

Appraise your own organisation's relationships with its suppliers. Are they adversarial, collaborative – or somewhere in-between?

What suppliers are used by the marketing function – and what type of relationships does it have with them?

What are the features and tools of collaborative supplier relationships, as practised in your organisation?

3 Demographic change

3.1 Consumer markets

It is easy to overlook demographics but demographics are important. We use demographics when building customer profiles and sometimes for segmenting markets. In Chapter 3 we used the example of the ageing UK population to consider how this might influence activity. In India the population profile is the reverse of the ageing population in the Western World.

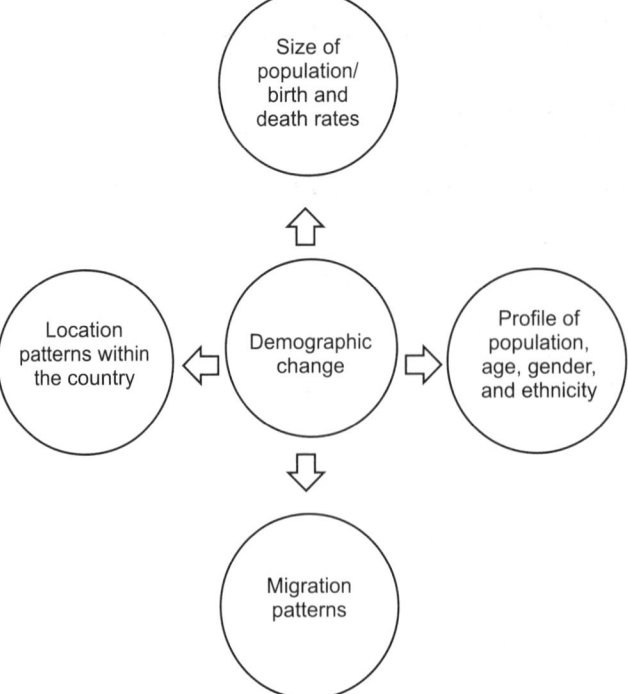

3.1.1 What about migration?

Would an increase in levels of immigration be a good or bad thing? A weakened UK economy with high levels of unemployment may make the UK a less attractive destination for economic migrants. There is evidence of Polish and other Eastern European workers quitting the UK, but what would the impact of this be?

ACTIVITY 10 application

Look up this article, by Danny Dorling on the Guardian website www.guardian.co.uk

http://www.guardian.co.uk/society/joepublic/2009/apr/23/migration-emigration-uk-dorling

The Guardian 23rd April 2009

Why low migration levels threaten the UK's economic and social health

The falling fertility rate and an ageing population mean that too little immigration may turn out to be a bigger problem for the UK than too much migration.

Danny Dorling, Professor of Human Geography at Sheffield University, has written a paper for the Institute for Public Policy Research project on the economics of migration.

Sources

The Institute for Public Policy Research is a leading and progressive think tank, producing cutting edge research and innovative policy ideas for a just, democratic and sustainable world.

Since 1988, it has been at the forefront of progressive debate and policymaking in the UK. Through independent research and analysis it defines new agendas for change and provide practical solutions to challenges across the full range of public policy issues.

3.2 Business markets

Demographics are not restricted to the consumer markets. Changes in the number of firms, their average size, location and sector are as equally valid and important if you are working in the business to business sector. These are structural changes that can have major implications for the success of nations and the performance of specific sectors. There is for example concern about London's ability to retain its prominence as a global financial service centre following the collapse of the banking systems globally and the UK's role in that.

Recession and high levels of unemployment are typically catalysts for increased business start ups and a boost to innovation.

 The Banks can be a useful source of information and data. Try www.business.barclays.co.uk

Statistics released by Barclays (2009) show that the number of new businesses set up during 2008 increased on 2007 levels, with female-run startups showing a 9% increase.

The estimated number of new enterprises formed last year rose from 432,300 in 2007 to 436,600 in 2008, with the overall number of businesses in the UK rising to around 2.9 million.

According to the Barclays data, the number of new businesses run solely by women increased by 9% to 90,000 last year, with male-only enterprises rising 1% to 300,0000.

 ACTIVITY 11 application

Take the time to find out how the demographics of your sector have changed recently. Your trade association or sector bodies may be a useful starting point.

To find a relevant trade association you could try the UK Trade Association Forum. The website can be found at www.taforum.org.

4 Social and cultural change

Social and cultural changes go straight to the heart of customer needs and behaviours. Changes here can directly impact on the basis of market segmentation and the ways in which organisations engage with their markets.

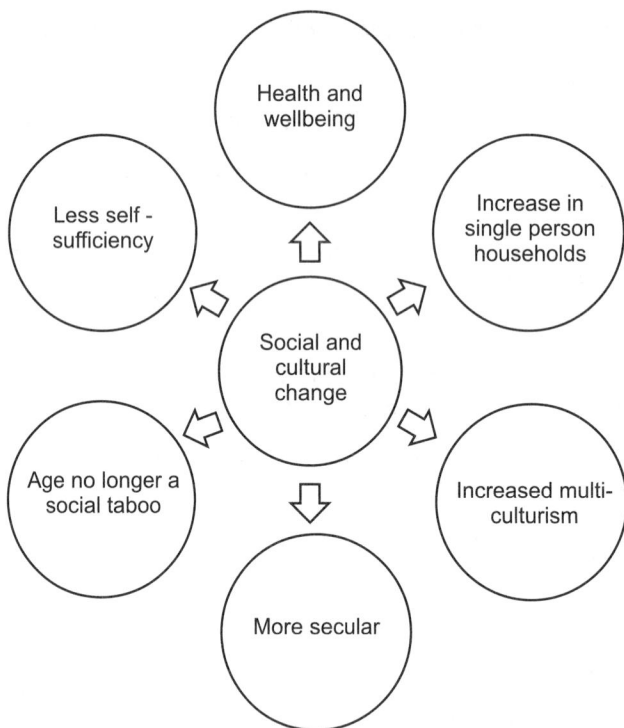

4.1 More single person households

In Chapter 3 we considered the issue of childhood health and obesity in some detail and also the impact of the ageing population with the resulting increased social acceptability of being over 60.

In this section we shall examine a further example of an emerging theme, that of the increase in single person households.

Below is an extract from a report *Single person households and social policy: Looking forwards* by Jim Bennett and Mike Dixon published by the Joseph Rowntree Foundation (April 2006). You can find more details and read the report summary in full at the Institute of Public Policy Research.

- The rise in solo living has been one of the most important demographic shifts of recent decades.
- There have been four key trends which will continue over the next decades:
    - elderly people, particularly women are the most likely group to live alone;
    - the fastest growth in solo living is amongst people aged 25 and 44;
    - growth in solo living has been fastest among young men;
    - solo living is becoming more permanent, particularly for men.

People living alone can be usefully split into two types:

- **Elective** single person households who have chosen solo living
- **Forced** single person households who have been constrained to this lifestyle by circumstances

There are implications and opportunities for many sectors in meeting the needs of this growing group.

A Data Monitor Report – '*Targeting the needs of single households*' estimates 1/3rd of all Europeans live alone and they spend 13% more than the average two person unit on food, drink and personal care. They represent a market in these sectors worth an estimated 880 million euros.

You can access the Data monitor report at:
www.datamonitor.com/Products/Free/Report/DMCM0414/010DMCM0414.pdf

What are the emerging themes resulting from this trend? The Joseph Rowntree Research identifies a number of implications for neighbourhoods, social capital and health.

- City centres may become increasingly dominated by people living alone, but there is little evidence that the increased popularity of city centre living is creating benefits for deprived inner urban areas.
- Increasing solo living may lead to greater isolation and worse physical and mental health for some groups, particularly men.
- There is some evidence that the growth in solo living could be '*harnessed*' to improve levels of social capital if policy can respond appropriately.
- Single person households are more vulnerable to crime; as more people live alone, there may be greater demand for victim support services and police protection.
- A significant proportion of single person households will be estranged fathers. Their ability to engage in the upbringing of their children may be hindered by their low priority for housing and social welfare.

Attitudes and needs of this group will be important to understand if business is to address them effectively.

4.2 An example

Swedish management guru Kjell Nordström highlights the additional strains these single person households are having on Europe's Health Services. If living alone and feeling unwell there is a greater likelihood the person will ring a doctor or call an ambulance – services like NHS Direct can help counter this demand with reassurance by phone.

5 Technological change

You will have your own list of technological changes likely to drive the next generation of emerging themes. Your list might include solar energy or wave technology. We have picked out a few in our overview below.

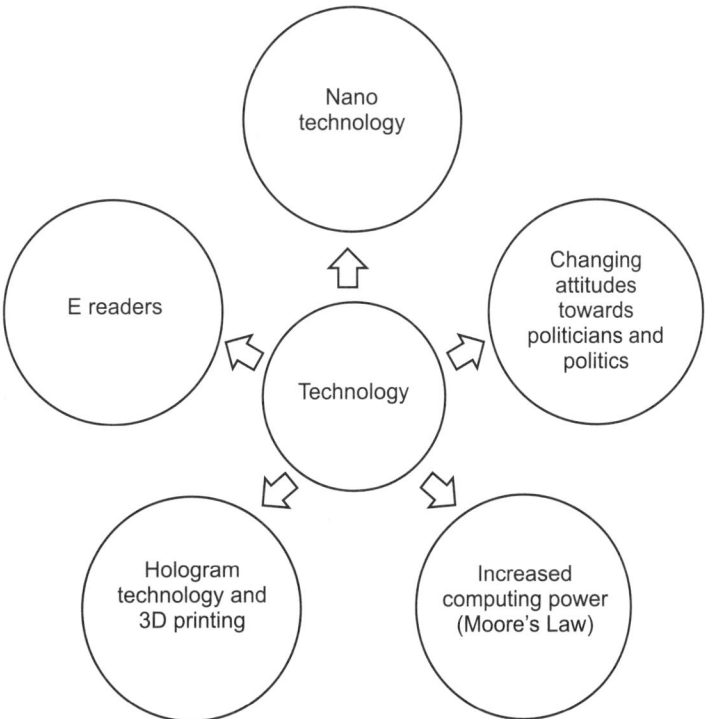

5.1 Nanotechnology and 3D printing

Nanotechnology, shortened to "**Nanotech**", is the study of the control of matter on an atomic and molecular scale and involves developing materials or devices within that size. It is sometimes referred to as a '*general-purpose technology*'. That's because in its advanced form it will have significant impact on almost all industries and all areas of society. It will offer better built, longer lasting, cleaner, safer, and smarter products for the home, communications, medicine, transportation, agriculture, and industry in general.

"Imagine a medical device that travels through the human body to seek out and destroy small clusters of cancerous cells before they can spread. Or, a box no larger than a sugar cube that contains the entire contents of the Library of Congress. Or, materials much lighter than steel that possess ten times as much strength." U.S. National Science Foundation (2009).

ACTIVITY 12

application

A visit to You Tube

Find out more about nanotechnology on You Tube (www.youtube.com).

For an overview of the world of these very small developments use the search term '*Nanotechnology Takes Off - KQED* QUEST

You should also watch *Nokia Morph Concept* (long), one of a number of Nokia clips. This one takes a look at how nanotechnology might change the world of communication.

You might also take a sneak preview at the world of 3D printing. Visit www.clipser.com and search for '*3D printing*'. You will find a number of clips that show you how this technology might revolutionise product development and communication. The barriers to technology access could be removed with individuals able to print their own developed products from a cocktail glass to an ipod cover or watch strap.

What would be the implications for your sector?

5.2 The E-reader and the Newspaper sector

E-readers are handheld devices that allow you to read books in digital format – e-books

They are about the size of regular books and use '*electronic paper*' to simulate the experience of traditional reading; text is set out on '*pages*' that you '*turn*' rather than scroll through (indeed you may even be reading this text as an e-book!).

It is thought that what the iPod did for the music industry e-books will do for the publishing world. E-book technology will do the same for the newspaper and magazine industry, currently suffering badly in the recession.

The latest emerging development for this technology is portable reading devices with big screens.

Unlike tiny mobile phones these new gadgets have screens roughly the size of a standard sheet of paper. The devices could present much of the editorial and advertising content of traditional periodicals in generally the same format as they appear in print. They might also be a way to get readers to pay for those periodicals — something they have been reluctant to do on the Web.

Such devices offer an almost irresistible proposition to newspaper and magazine industries. They would allow publishers to save millions on the cost of printing and distributing their publications, at precisely a time when their businesses are under historically high levels of pressure.

They represent a chance for this sector to rethink its strategy of free content via the internet. Subscription models are already being considered by News Corporation – with Rupert Murdoch making it clear that he thinks the current business models for the news industry are flawed.

The question we need to consider is how easy it will be to get the consumer to accept paying for content they have got used to accessing free. Websites like the BBC provide what may appear *free* but in effect is a subscription service paid for by the annual licence fee.

5.3 Technology and the consumers' response

The consumer is increasingly conversant with the world of technology and what it can do for him/her. We are adopting new technology more quickly (as long as we can see the benefits it offers). There have been some examples, for instance GM crops, which show customers will reject technology they feel may not be safe. This has significant implications for the positioning and marketing of new technology.

There is data available to help you assess the take up and use of technology:

In 2009, 18.3 million households in Great Britain (70 per cent) had internet access. This is an increase of just over 2 million households (11 per cent) since 2008 and 4 million households (28 per cent) since 2006.

(Source: /www.statistics.gov.uk)

6 The environment

The environment is a topic that has attracted considerable media and popular interest. The rise of the 'green consumer' has been a trend that has been observable for many years. It is closely linked to the response from business in the form of Corporate Social Responsibility strategies which we will be considering in the next chapter. An overview of some of the key macro trends under the environment heading includes:

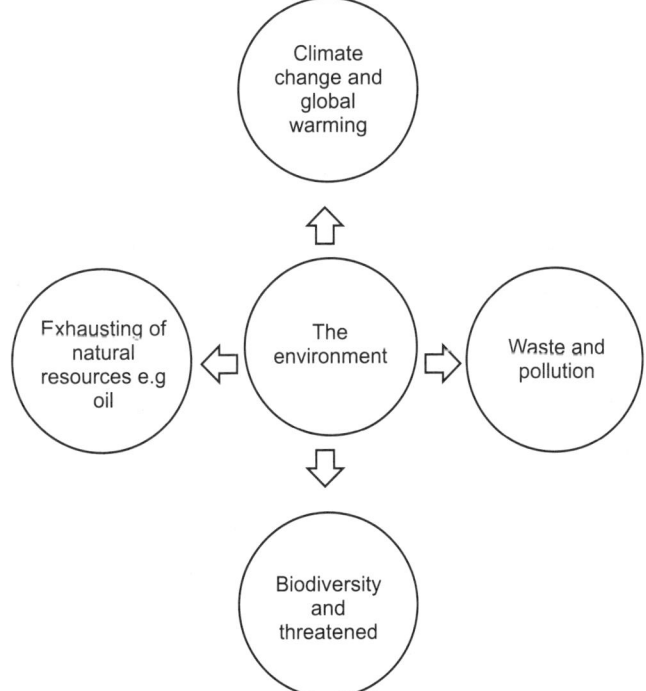

6.1 Climate change

This is one of the biggest changes with implications for how we live and work.

  ACTIVITY 13  evaluation

Weather Forecast

Find out about the forecast changes on www.bbc.co.uk/climate and then tackle the questions below.

Whilst visiting the site take the time to listen to and review the content about the UKC1PO2 scenarios. These are real examples of scenario planning in practice with a 100 year planning horizon.

(a) What is the greenhouse effect?

(b) What are the UKCIP02 scenarios and what do they say?

(c) What would be the potential impact of increased precipitation?

(d) What opportunities would a warmer UK offer?

(e) What are some of the key changes you may expect to emerge from the real concerns about the climate?

(f) Why might roofs need to change?

6.2 Waste and pollution

This aspect of environmental concerns is of direct concern to marketers who may be responsible for packaging decisions.

According to a YouGov poll, in 2008 we got through 9.9 billion bags, which equates to 162 bags per person and is enough to fill 188 Olympic-sized swimming pools. They only account for 3.5 to 5.3 per cent of the total plastic packaging used but they are everywhere and take 400 years to break down.

Changing customer behaviour is possible. Some countries are making it a political decision with taxes and bans – others are relying on the retailers to 'market' the behaviour change to customers. In Ireland a tax on plastic bags in 2002 resulted in the number of plastic bags given out dropping by 90 per cent in just 1 year.

San Francisco and Paris have already banned plastic carrier bags. So has the Devon town of Modbury.

In 2006, the Australian state of Victoria became the first on the continent to ban free plastic bags.

Further afield, China banned shops from handing out free plastic bags in June 2008.

In April 2009, as part of the Government and the British Retail Consortium's *'Get a bag habit'* campaign, UK's leading seven supermarkets made a further commitment to halve the number of bags they give away by the end of May 2009.

(Source: www.bbc.co.uk/food/foodmatters/packaging, 2009)

 MARKETING AT WORK application

The UK has relied on retailer actions rather than taxation. When Sainsbury's launched the cotton *'I am not a plastic bag'* carrier designed by Anya Hindmarch in April 2007 as an alternative to plastic bags, there were queues for a style accessory that became a collector's item.

- In February 2008 Marks & Spencer began charging customers 5p per plastic bag, with the money raised going to an environmental charity.

- In 2007, Asda agreed to cut packaging by 25 per cent on its own-brand packaging by 2008.

- Co-op introduced the first biodegradable carrier bag in 2002 and uses degradable netting and trays for some of its organic fruit and vegetables.

- By 2012 Marks & Spencer says all its packaging will be recyclable or compostable.
- Morrisons introduced compostable packaging to its own-brand organic produce in 2007.
- Tesco's less ambitious target is to reduce by 25 per cent packaging on own-brand and branded products by 2010.
- Sainsbury's is stepping up the proportion of fruit and vegetables it sells loose and pledged to reduce by 25 per cent the amount of packaging on fruit and vegetables by 2008. Its new carrier bags are made with one-third recycled material.
- Waitrose introduced the reusable '*bag for life*' in 1997 (customers buy a bag for 10p, which is replaced for free when it wears out. Returned 'bags for life' are recycled into furniture). 50 per cent of its organic range of fresh produce is available in degradable, biodegradable and compostable packaging.

6.2.1 The recession and waste

There is already evidence that the recession is having a stronger impact on our behaviour as we are being extolled to:

- **Reduce** – for example '*Love Food Hate Waste*' campaign', launched by the government watchdog Waste Resources and Action Programme (Wrap) in November 2007, has raised awareness of the £10.2bn of food waste we throw away each year.
- **Reuse**
- **Re-cycle** – Defra's figures show a surge in recycling. Britons recycled 36.3 per cent of their rubbish last year, up from 30.9 per cent in 2007.

Local councils and waste management companies across the whole country are reporting a drop of up to 10 per cent in waste collection in recent months, a fall that the UK environmental charity Waste Watch estimates could result in a massive reduction of 2.5 million tonnes in waste production in 2009 – enough rubbish to fill Canary Wharf five times over.

A number of factors have contributed to this:

- The shift in public attitudes away from profligate living and the disposable economy
- A drop in the amount of white goods, such as washing machines and TVs, being thrown out
- A fall in construction waste, as the recession affects the number of building projects.

Again the question is how sustainable is this trend? To maintain this fall there is a need to decouple economic growth from waste growth (which may be less easy to achieve).

 ACTIVITY 14   evaluation

Before you move on to the next chapter and a look at the emerging themes take time to apply your macro level thinking to your own sector. Create your map of the key macro trends driving your sector and note any useful sources of information that will help you assess these.

Learning objective review

Learning objectives	Covered
1 Changes in political governance systems and political focus.	☑ Changing political attitude
	☑ Changing political climate
	☑ Devolution
	☑ Legal environment
	☑ Marketers and the law
2 Contemporary economic opportunities and challenges	☑ An economic overview
	☑ The recession and its impact at sector and customer level
	☑ The implications for marketers
	☑ Network governance
3 Demographic change	☑ For consumer markets – migration
	☑ For business markets
4 Social change at local and global levels	☑ More single person households
	☑ (Note ageing population and childhood obesity covered in Chapter 3)
5 Emerging technologies	☑ Nanotechnology and 3D printing
	☑ The e-reader and the newspaper sector
	☑ Technology and the consumers' response
6 Environmental challenges	☑ Climate change
	☑ Waste and pollution

Quick quiz

1. Will increased devolution make it easier or harder for firms working with the public sector?
2. Is the current political climate more or less likely to favour greater devolution?
3. Would you expect public sector spending to increase or fall in most countries over the next few years?
4. What might be the impact on Health Services of a continued growth in the number of single person households?
5. What change might 3D printing make to innovation and the location of production?
6. Which sectors may benefit from UK climate change?
7. How is recession helping deliver the 'green' agenda?
8. Why is it important for marketers to understand the implications of these major macro-environmental trends?

1-2   These activities will depend on your own research

3   **Legal changes that have had an impact**

Our list includes:

- Banning smoking in public places which has had a significant negative impact on the pub industry and certainly contributed to an estimated closure of 5 pubs a week in 2008.

- The London Olympic Games and Paralympic Games Act 2006 which specifies that only companies which have been awarded official sponsorship status can make explicit reference to the Olympics in their promotions. According to a CIM poll, some 40% of marketers surveyed were unaware of the provisions of the Act or the potential £20,000 fine. To prevent ambush marketing and to protect exclusivity of official sponsors, the organiser of the Games, The London Organising Committee of the Olympic Games Limited (LOCOG), trading as *'London 2012',* has special statutory marketing rights under The London Olympics Association Right. It also has special legal rights under The London Olympic Games and Paralympic Games Act 2006 and The Olympic Symbol etc (Protection) Act 1995.

- Data protection legislation which has had considerable implications for what data companies hold about customers and how they use that information.

- Freedom of Information Act which has opened up a number of areas of government to scrutiny and so has been a catalyst for improved governance.

- A raft of Health and Safety legislation which has impacted many sectors and influenced the environments in which customers can interact with organisations.

4-7   These activities will depend on your own research

8   **Recession Hits Retail in South Africa**

- They need to focus on retaining customers who may be lured away by price promotions from desperate competitors during this time. Customers could be expected to be more promiscuous and cautious. Shopping around will be more likely so strategies for retention and rewarding loyalty need to be a cornerstone. Retailers might look at ways that current loyal customers can be encouraged to become advocates for the business – '*introduce a friend* ' type schemes. Those customers who have recession-based problems need help. Meeting their needs with economy solutions should help retain their current reduced spend but also will build a longer-term and deeper relationship with them. Finally there will be opportunities to win new customers. Those who pre-recession were buying from a more expensive supplier will potentially '*trade-down*'. In the UK Lidl and ASDA are doing well as non-traditional customers discover what they have to offer.

- Some people within a market will do better than others. Those with mortgages and debts may be benefiting from lower interest payments, whilst those living off savings may be seeing their income levels fall. Whatever behavioural or demographic variables have been used to segment the market pre-recession that now needs to be overlaid by a recession factor.

- Value is key but retailers should take care with straight price cuts – the 50% off approach may soon become expected and has the ability to trigger further price wars in the sector. Package deals ....a meal for £x are more appealing and provide the opportunity for much more creativity and innovation. Promotions to encourage repeat visits and loyalty would also be attractive.

- Retailers should look at promotional activity, considering less use of broadcast media and looking for new media opportunities, networking and below the line through events etc. The extent to which this will be effective will depend on the penetration of new media in the South African market but mobile phones ownership could for example make SMS campaigns announcing '*this week's offer*' an option.

9   Your own research. Note that your findings may be useful preparation for an assignment task.

10-12   These activities will depend on your own organisation.

13 **Weather forecast**

(a) The greenhouse effect is at the centre of the climate change debate. The sun warms the earth and in turn a warm earth radiates its own rays. Those rays that don't escape past the atmosphere are absorbed by the greenhouse gases. These create the temperatures we experience today.

(b) These represent four different scenarios for UK climate change over the next 100 years. They take account of technology and lifestyle changes and look at scenarios for low, medium, medium high and high emissions. The degree of difference forecast depends on the level of emissions the scenario is based upon.

(c) More risk of flooding with implications on urban development, house buildings and insurance. We would see different animals and plants.

(d) Outdoor activities, at least in the summer, would be more attractive (and reliable). We will be able to produce more wine and may well attract more tourists. A summer beach holiday in the UK will grow in appeal as hotter countries get too hot to be comfortable.

(e) Increasing use and development of renewable energy. Individual responsibility for energy could be an emerging trend. April 2009 saw the announcement of SMART meters that provide households with considerable detail of energy use over time. New houses may be expected to incorporate many new features and materials.

(f) Weather conditions may require pitch and overlap of roof tiles to change to cope with stronger winds and increased rainfall.

14 This activity will depend on your own sector

Quiz answers

1 It will make it more difficult as policy and priorities will be made at local level. However it will also allow more firms to potentially win public contracts and could mean better prices and terms are negotiated benefiting margins.

2 It is more likely to favour it. People upset by the allowances and expenses scandal at Westminster will prefer more local projects where how money is spent will be more transparent.

3 You would expect it to fall, due to a combination of factors. These would include lower levels of economic activity following the recession plus the need to repay the debt generated by the various bail out and rescue activities.

4 Increased pressure on health services. Single households often have poorer health and little '*care*' at home.

5 It will encourage innovation at the household level. People will be able to design and produce products for themselves – a return to 'cottage industry'.

6 Wine making and tourism will be amongst the winners.

7 People are spending less on consumer goods, there is less building activity, and a reduction in waste as '*thrifty*' habits replace more profitable ones.

8 Because these changes will shape the needs of customers in the future and marketers need to be alert to them and their potential implications to '*future proof*' strategy.

References

Barclays (2009) *"Economic outlook"* available online at: http://www.business.barclays.co.uk/BRC1/jsp/brccontrol?task=homefreevi6&site=bbb&value=9034&menu=4597 [accessed 21st June 2009].

BBC (2009) *"Packaging"* available online at: http://www.bbc.co.uk/food/food_matters/packaging2.shtml [accessed 21st June 2009].

Bennett, J. and Dixon, M (2006) Single person households and social policy: Looking forwards , Joseph Rowntree Foundation.

Datamonitor (2003) "*Targeting the needs of people who live alone*" report available online at: www.datamonitor.com/Products/Free/Report/DMCM0414/010DMCM0414.pdf [accessed 21st June 2009].

Dorling, D (2009) "*Why low migration levels threaten the UK's economic and social health*" The Guardian, London, 23rd April 2009.

Namnews (2009) *"Recession fears loom as retail sales drop in March"* available online at: http://namnews.com/namnews/asp/newsarticle.asp?newsid=47385 [accessed 20th May 2009].

Northern Ireland Omnibus Survey (2009) Survey summary available online at http://www.csu.nisra.gov.uk/survey.asp10.htm [accessed 21st June 2009].

US National Science Foundation (2009) Nanotechnology Initiatives available online at: http://www.nsf.gov/crssprgm/nano/ [accessed 21st June 2009].

Wikipedia (2009) "*Devolution*" available online at: http://en.wikipedia.org/wiki/Devolution [accessed 21st June 2009].

Chapter 5
Emerging themes within organisations

Topic list

1. Marketing's new ground
2. New skills for tomorrow's marketers
3. Corporate Social Responsibility
4. Business Ethics

Introduction

This chapter takes economic or industry trends and assesses what is happening within businesses or organisations. There are numerous strands and themes which could be considered but for this chapter we will focus on just a few (in detail) to illustrate the way in which implications can be developed and assessed.

Syllabus linked learning objectives

By the end of the chapter you will be able to:

Learning objectives	Syllabus link
1 Describe how marketing's role in business is changing and '*scope*' this new world for marketing	2.1, 2.2, 2.3
2 Recommend ways in which marketers need to build new skills and approaches to fulfilling this changing role.	2.1, 2.2, 2.3
3 Discuss some of the '*new*' strategies being followed by business and consider the implications of these.	2.1, 2.2, 2.3
4 Assess a specific emerging issue, assess its impacting on a specific organisation and use scenario planning to help 'vision' different futures and consider the implications on a specific organisation.	2.1, 2.2, 2.3

1 Marketing's new ground

Throughout this module the more strategic role for marketing has been implicit. In this chapter we will be making that strategic role more explicit.

As market conditions have changed so there is a need to change business strategy and therefore the orientation of business. When demand exceeds supply you have a 'sellers' market and the need for, and role of, marketing is negligible.

- As demand and supply '*equalise*' so businesses must be more pro-active in seeking customers for their products and services. This creates a sales orientation and marketing is used predominantly for sales support. This operational focus is usually built around hitting short-term sales targets and therefore filling the sales funnel. Marketing at this stage is really marketing communication.

- Only when organisations find themselves in '*buyers' markets*', where supply exceeds demand does a customer orientation become critical to success. Marketers end up taking a much more strategic role – helping ensure the organisation develops and delivers products and services that meet/exceed customer needs. The new role of marketing is the '*architect of competitive advantage*'. Marketers have responsibility to use their insight into emerging and changing customer needs to help shape the way the organisations will '*compete*' for those customers.

This is a role which is as much about research and external monitoring as it is about communication and prioritisation.

You can consider marketers to be '*customer experts*' and advocates or as the communication centre for the business, listening as well as telling customers.

The following diagram puts this notion into contect.

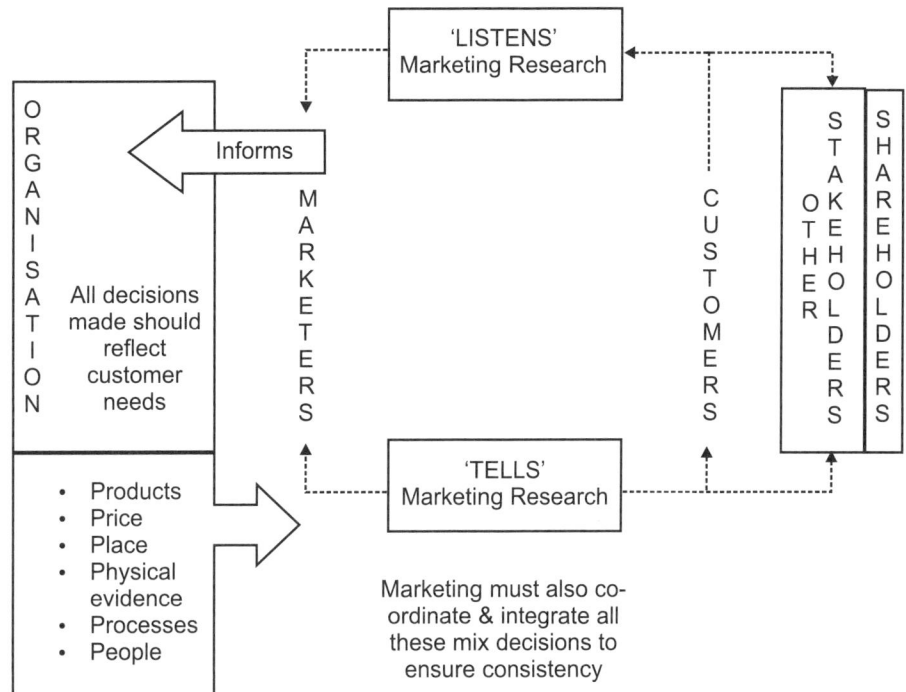

Source: Angela Hatton (2000)

 ACTIVITY 1   evaluation

How do you see marketers' role emerging?

Use this diagram as a framework for assessing the new role of marketing.

What do you feel would be the main issues, challenges or responsibilities at points 1-4?

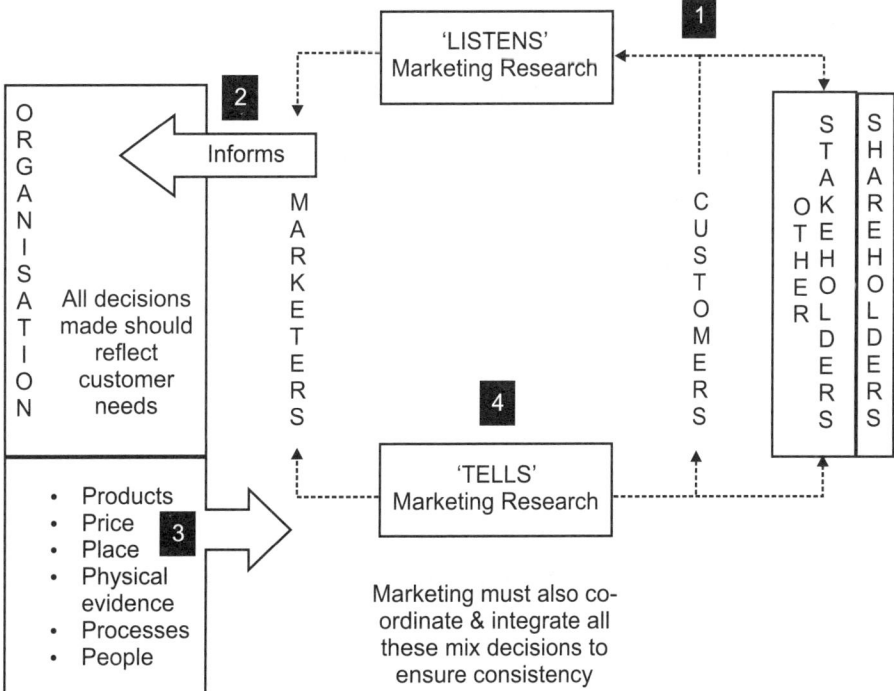

5: Emerging themes within organisations

Marketers' role will be:

(1)

(2)

(3)

(4)

Compare your thoughts with ours provided at the end of this Chapter.

1.1 The changing role of marketing

As the orientation and strategy of business has evolved so has the role of marketing within the business.

The emerging themes in this changing role are summarised below:

(a) **More strategic**, though still with operational responsibilities. You would expect to see marketing matters on the board room agenda with discussions about retention levels and acquisition rates, market share, average customer value and share of wallet and the return on marketing investment. These are the 'lead' metrics that are indicators of changing competitive advantage and so are early indicators of strategic wearout or improving competitive performance. You might expect to see Marketing managers in the Boardroom to represent this critical agenda.

(b) **More holistic** refers to the fact that what we call the marketing mix, the 7 P's, are not directly controlled by marketers. They may be better described as the business mix. Therefore marketing must work with professional colleagues and third party suppliers to ensure all aspects of the offer are aligned to deliver customer value. This more business wide role requires a more holistic approach.

(c) Marketing's role will be **re-positioned** and seen not just as communications or sales support but acknowledged as the key value driver for the business. This role will lead to greater respect for marketing and the insight it brings about what customers (and other stakeholders) need and value. There will increasingly be an organisation-wide understanding of why customer focus matters and how spending on marketing drives long term shareholder value, building intangible assets through the brand and customer goodwill.

(d) Marketing is evolving steadily from an art characterised by intuitive '*gut*' feel decision making, to more of a **science with decisions** based on detailed analysis and increased objectivity. Marketers expect to have to make and argue the business case behind their proposals and recommendations.

(e) Being in the boardroom means being able to **communicate in the financial language of the boardroom**. Marketers must understand shareholder value, return on investment and assess the financial implications of their recommendations because decisions about the mix of customers, products and the marketing mix all impact the bottom line of the business.

1.2 Our role will keep on changing

In the diagram in Activity 1 we are considering the role of marketers in an environment where business success depends on delivering customer satisfaction more effectively than the competitors. Essentially a process of mutually profitable exchange:

- Satisfied customers
- Generates improving business performance

However we have already investigated some of the emerging themes that are impacting on business strategy and so the role of marketers. These are the themes which have broadened the business agenda and include the satisfaction of other stake holders.

Corporate social responsibility (CSR) broadens the role of marketing still further. The question of the employees and employee brand, community and financial media relations and lobbying industry regulators could all appear on that agenda.

The questions which may need to be considered are to what extent marketers will control or even take a lead in this broader agenda.

 ## ACTIVITY 2

evaluation

Who else may be involved?

Take a few moments to consider this broader stakeholder agenda. What other groups of professionals might be involved in a broader CSR strategy or agenda?

Check your thoughts with ours at the end of the chapter.

You can see that an emerging theme for marketers may be the need to work much more collaboratively with these other professional colleagues to ensure CSR initiatives are integrated and the '*brand*' is managed constantly across all stakeholder audiences.

 ## ACTIVITY 3

application

Assessing the current role of marketing in your organisation

Read one of CIM's Shape the Agenda papers *'Tomorrow's World'* which looks at how marketing has changed over the past 30 years and makes some predictions for its role and structure in the future strategies that encompass environmental sensibility and social awareness. You can assess this article on CIM's website.

Those in B2B companies may still find themselves in a '*sales and marketing*' team with responsibility predominantly for sales support. Increased competition and the reality of a buyers' market will be the catalysts that change marketing's role. Wherever you are on that journey you and your team need to:

- Ensure you have developed your own skills so you can take that more strategic role
- Be able to make the business case to support that new emerging role for marketing

2 New skills for tomorrow's marketers

You will already have seen how these emerging agendas will impact on the job roles of marketing professionals. You would certainly expect the job description of 10 years ago to look different to a description today.

It is because the role and expectations of marketing are changing that marketing teams need to take pro-active steps to ensure they are continually developing their own skills and capabilities in order to rise to these new challenges. The role of Continuing Professional Development (CPD) and encouraging those entering marketing to become professionally qualified are cornerstones for the ongoing learning marketing teams must do.

The following diagram summarises the new skills required.

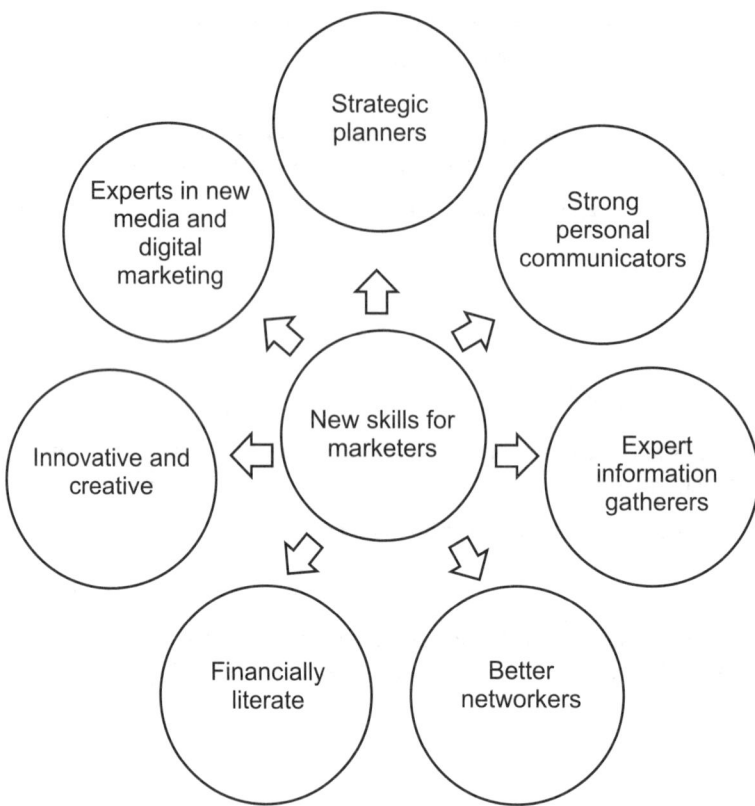

Your own analysis of the new skills needed will depend on the current role of marketing and the type of sector you operate in. For those working globally the need for language skills may feature.

 ASSIGNMENT TIP  concept

For the assignment for this module you will be required to identify and evaluate one or two emerging themes considering how they will impact on your sector and or organisation. You need to also consider and make explicit:

- The implications for marketers
- What they need to do differently
- What new skills may need to be developed as a result of this '*emerging theme*'.

  ACTIVITY 4 evaluation

How creative are you?

You might like to take this opportunity to assess just how creative you and your marketing colleagues are.

Try these online quizzes:

(a)   Developed by Professor Brian Uzzi at Kello Northwestern University:

   http://www.kellogg.northwestern.edu/faculty/uzzi/ftp/page176.html

(b)   Just for fun try

   http://www.blogthings.com/howcreativearyouquiz

ASSIGNMENT TIP

Take time at your next team meeting to discuss how well you are prepared to meet the emerging themes facing your organisation. Complete a strengths and weaknesses analysis, prioritising those new skills which you feel will be most important to future performance in your sector. Talk to HR and decide how you can take steps to improve performance in the important areas where you feel there are weaknesses in your skills.

Importance to performance in your sector	Strength			Weakness	
	+10	+5	0	-5	-10
Very important					
Important					
Less important					

2.1 The key strategies for business

How companies compete for customers and succeed in achieving their stakeholders' agenda is changing and will continue to change in response to the themes and trends we have been examining in this module.

Which strategies are most important to you depends to a large extent on the sector you are working in but being alert and forward looking will be critical to long term success.

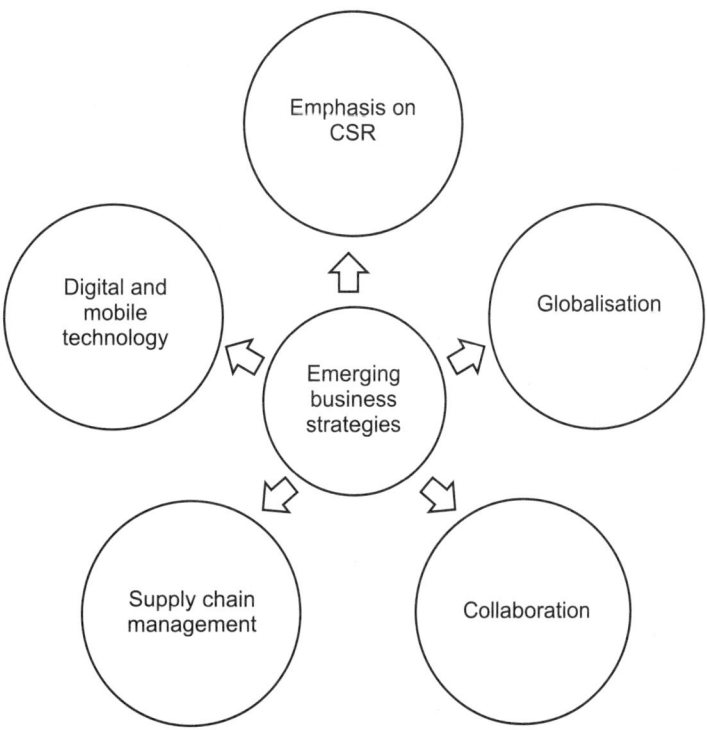

5: Emerging themes within organisations

Utalkmarketing.com is the first free community site for marketers, by marketers.

Its mission is to fuel passion for marketing by bringing the latest news to inform marketers, ads to inspire you, forums and comment to challenge you.

Register for their early morning briefings to find out what is happening in a range of sectors and remember you can learn a lot by applying the learning from one sector to your sector.

Utalkmarketing says it has 120,000 marketers already using the site and their daily briefing is often interesting – providing information that will help you identify and evaluate emerging themes.

UTalkMarketing is a privately funded company backed by The Creative Capital Fund which launched in January 2007. It is led by Niall McKinney, who has worked in marketing in the UK for the last nine years. Niall previously worked at Procter & Gamble, and at IPC Media, where he was Publishing and Marketing Director. Most recently he was Chief Marketing Officer of Lastminute.com across Europe

3 Corporate Social Responsibility

CSR has been a recurring theme in this module – not surprisingly when you consider how much is written about the environment, pollution and sustainability.

Even within this area you can see there are many aspects, themes and dimensions that need to be assessed and considered.

Let's start by looking at CSR and business strategy – how might an organisation audit its current CSR stand or identify further opportunities to strengthen its CSR policies and strategies.

This value chain model has been populated with top level implications /or options for a CSR approach.

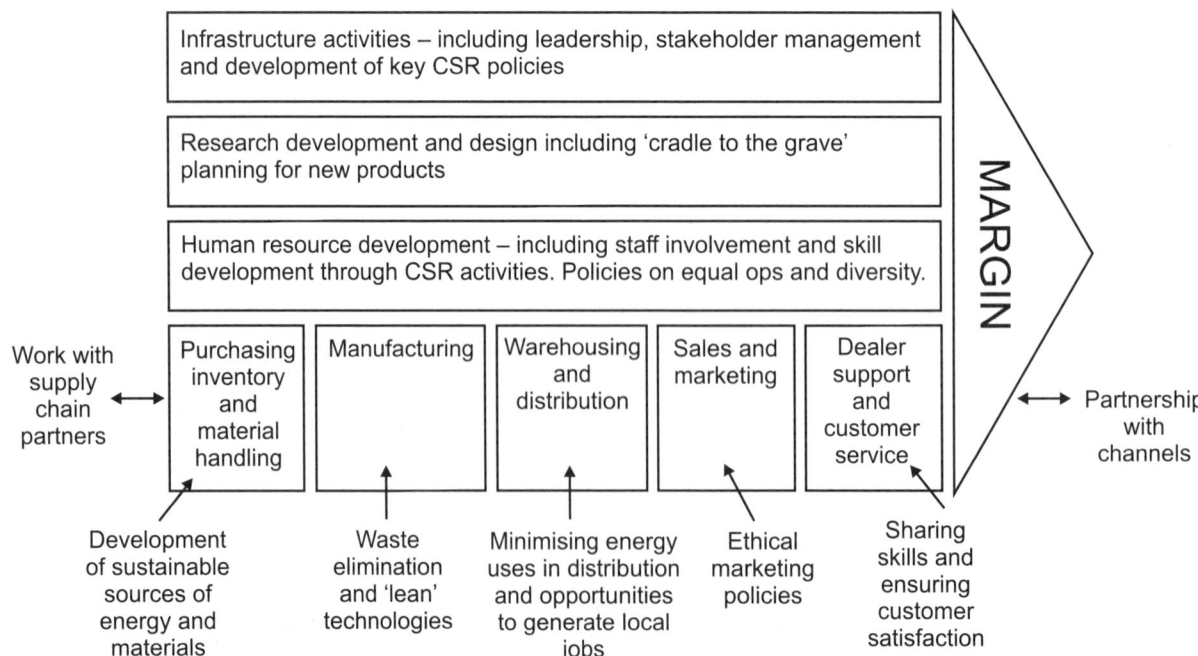

Note that in this case '*margin*' would not just be financial margin but would need to measure improved performance against the three dimensions of the triple bottom line.

Three areas of economic, social and environmental considerations are important to CSR.

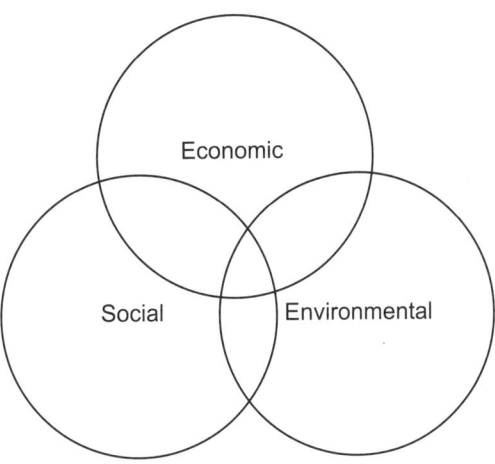

You will find a lot of companies are very explicit about their CSR strategies so you can find out quite a lot from their web sites.

 MARKETING AT WORK   application

Social Responsibility at B&Q

'Since 1990 B&Q have taken a positive approach to the challenges that social responsibility presents and have developed solutions that not only address our environmental and social impacts but also add value to our business and its reputation.

B&Q's core values include:

Environment

Every product we sell at B&Q has its own unique life cycle or story. As such we have a responsibility to ensure that any possible environmental impact is as low as possible during manufacture, use and disposal.

Ethical Trading

It is our duty to ensure that everyone involved in B&Q supply chains benefits from trading with us. Our customers want great products at great prices, but not at the expense of the people who make them. We are committed to sourcing products responsibly.

Diversity

At B&Q we are committed to eliminating all forms of discrimination and ensuring an inclusive environment irrespective of age, gender, marital or civil partnership status, colour, ethnic or national origin, culture, religion, religious belief or similar philosophical belief, disability, political affiliation, gender identity, gender reassignment or sexual orientation.

Community

We have a significant influence on the communities in which we operate, and our aim is for all our stores to be welcomed as 'good neighbours' in the communities that they serve, including the contribution of skills and funding to selected community projects.'

Visit the B&Q web site at *www.diy.com,* calculate your personal eco-footprint and carbon emissions with their one planet living footprint calculator and look at the customer advice they are providing to help educate their customers about the environment and its resources.

B&Q has been working with award-winning environmental charity BioRegional to develop an extensive range of one planet home® independently accredited products. One planet living® is a lifestyle where we can all enjoy an excellent quality of life while staying within our fair share of the earth's resources. They provide advice on saving energy, water, recycling and growing your own.

How do your CSR policies and strategies compare? What changes might happen over coming years? Use the value chain approach to help your assessment.

ACTIVITY 5

evaluation

About sustainability

To illustrate the range of converging themes and issues covered within CSR we can take just one aspect – sustainability and analyse just what that covers and means.

Sustainability is used frequently in the media and by marketers in their discussions about CSR and the ethics of their organisation. But what does it include?

Spend a few minutes thinking about sustainability – what topics would you include if you were speaking about the question in the context of your sector and business activities?

You can compare your list with ours at the end of this chapter.

3.1 Water shortage

Let's consider the emerging issue of water shortage. In the UK we tend to take water for granted – it has often felt like it is '*free at the point of delivery*' so we do not value it as we might. If you had to walk two miles to fetch water and carry it home you may use less of it to clean your teeth. Not all households are yet on water meters. But what we use in the home is only half the story. How much water do we 'eat'?

Water is used in almost every stage of food production, from growing crops to feed animals to washing and preparing products. Researchers at Cranfield University have calculated just how much water is used to produce many common foods:

- Cup of tea – 32.4 litres
- Pint of beer – 160 litres
- 1 glass of wine – 120 litres
- 1 glass of milk – 200 litres
- 1kg of beef – 15,000 litres
- 1kg poultry – 6,000 litres
- 250g packet of peanut M&Ms – 1,153 litres
- 575g Dolmio pasta sauce – 202 litres

Speaking at a meeting of the British Hydrological Society in March 2009 Mr Hess said few consumers were aware of just how much water is used to produce food, with a typical balanced diet requiring 3,500 litres of water per person per day.

"*Everything that we eat has consumed water in its production, from the water used to grow wheat for a loaf of bread, right down to the water used to grow crops for animal feed to produce meat for the supermarket shelves.*

We know that in the future the population will increase and the demand for food will increase. If the demand for food increases then the demand for water will increase and so water could become a major limiting factor on global production."

(Source: Davies, 2009)

Now let's look at what may be happening to water resources worldwide.

Analysts see widespread conflicts by 2015 but pin hopes on technology and better management

According to analysts working for Shell, Coca-Cola, Procter & Gamble, Cargill and other companies which depend heavily on secure water supplies, the next 20 years would be critical as countries became richer, making heavier demands on scarce water supplies.

The World Business Council on Sustainable Development brought the industrial groups together and took three years to complete the study of future water availability. Their analysis concludes that:

- *Conflicts are likely to become common in many countries*
- *Cholera may return to London*
- *Mass migration of Africans could cause civil unrest in Europe*
- *China's economy could crash by 2015*

as the supply of fresh water becomes critical to the global economy.

3.2 Back to scenario planning.

The group generated three future scenarios. As you will see the time horizons are not all that long and the implications fairly dramatic. The fact that we have now reached 2010 and some of the possible scenarios have not occurred, does not mean that the situation won't deteriorate in the future. If you were employed by a sector which needs secure water supplies what would you be saying?

Look at three scenarios below.

3.2.1 Scenario 1

Misery and shortages in the megacities and drought in Africa

By 2010, 22 megacities with populations larger than 10 million face major water and sewage problems. The situation is gravest in China, where 550 of the country's 600 largest towns and cities are running short. Growing demand for water by industry leads to serious over-exploitation with less and less water available for consumers and farmers. This leads to a fall in Chinese food production, which in turn leads to more imports and impacts on other countries. Friction and unrest grow worldwide as the middle classes struggle to pay bills. Businesses are exposed to charges of moral culpability and litigation over water use. Waves of immigrants flood into Europe from increasingly drought-torn Africa.

3.2.2 Scenario 2

China leads recycling rush as world moves to a new hydro economy

By 2010, the water shortage in many developing countries is one of the most serious political and social issues of the time. Lack of water is stopping development and in many countries the rural poor suffer as their water and other needs take second place to those of swelling cities and industry. Local government worldwide is increasingly distrusted over water allocation, and historical divides between rich and poor are exacerbated by water shortages. However, by 2025 a worldwide hydro economy is developing, led by China. Vast new investments are made in recycling water and the cost is greatly reduced. Innovative small-scale water treatment processes become the norm.

3.2.3 Scenario 3

Water is the means of social control as floods and disease devastate world

Water becomes a key symbol of protest around the world and is seen as the most serious social and political issue of the generation. By 2015, multinational companies are accused regularly of taking too much water in developing countries, cholera breaks out in London, and governments start to use water as a form of social control, subsidising some sectors and rationing it to others. Great floods follow each other in quick succession.

Deforestation leads to massive mudslides in Asia and increasing floods affect Europe, damaging industry. A second New Orleans flood devastates the city again. Global focus grows on the '*export*' of water via crops such as wheat or fruit.

ASSIGNMENT TIP

evaluation

Tutor Comment

Remember Gary Hamel's advice:

(a) Have foresight to vision the future
(b) Consider what you would need to do to compete in that future
(c) Build the capabilities and competencies you need to prepare for that future.

This structure may be a useful one to consider when planning your discussion paper for your assignment

ACTIVITY 6

evaluation

What should we do?

Take a few minutes to consider the three scenarios above. What would be the different implications of each for your business and what actions might you be recommending?

There is an example of how one company is responding in the feedback at the end of this chapter.

In the UK the Environment Agency (EA) published a new plan to tackle future water shortages, warning demand for water could increase by 25 per cent by 2020.

Andy Turner, head of water resources policy at the EA warned that demand for water in parts of the UK already outstrips that of many Mediterranean countries and it is likely to get worse with climate change.

Those areas of the country most at risk of water shortage are East Anglia and the Midlands, but with the effects of climate change the EA warned those shortages could move north and west affecting large swathes of England and Wales.

Publishing its 'Water Resources Strategy' for England and Wales, the EA set out measures that should be implemented to help protect water resources up to 2050, including:

- Introducing water meters for consumers.
- Placing a greater focus on conserving water in agriculture.
- Calling for greater investment in storage reservoirs in agriculture.
- Committing to working with Regional Development Agencies to fund new projects aimed at preserving water and maximising efficiency.
- Calling for the creation of more '*water abstraction groups*' where a group of farmers shares an abstraction licence and allocates water between its members.

The report calls for '*bold changes*' across a range of industries, and will now be passed on to various parts of government to help direct new policies aimed at preventing a water crisis.

MARKETING AT WORK

evaluation

The Environmental Agency is doing some social marketing activity to get the message across to farmers.

The 2009 Water Efficiency Awards

THE Environment Agency is currently inviting applications from farmers for its 2009 Water Efficiency Awards, recognising the role of business in promoting water efficiency.
Find out more by visiting www.water-efficiency-awards.org.uk.

What initiatives could be taken for your sector?

---

90 Emerging Themes

ASSIGNMENT TIP

Tutor Comment

Notice how by focusing on a very specific aspect of change you can be much more specific in your comments and it is likely your discussion paper for your assignment will be much more specific and powerful.

4 Business Ethics

A number of countries have an Institute of Business Ethics – you may like to Google IBE and make some comparisons of their agendas and concerns.

Let us take a look at another example of how business practice may be changing – the emerging theme is of increased ethics and morality in business and marketers have a considerable role to play.

According to Wikipedia:

Ethical marketing is an honest and factual representation of a product, delivered in a framework of cultural and social values for the consumer. It promotes qualitative benefits to its customers, which other similar companies, products or services fail to recognize. The concern with ethical issues, such as child labor, working conditions, relationships with third world countries and environmental problems, has changed the attitude of the Western World towards a more socially responsible way of thinking. This has influenced companies and their response is to market their products in a more socially responsible way.

KEY CONCEPT

According to the UK Institute of Business Ethics ethical marketing is '*the application of ethical values to business behaviour ...*'

In the UK the Institute of Business Ethics site contains lots of useful material for reviewing and monitoring this aspect of CSR. www.ibe.org.uk/"

This is what they have to say about the subject of business ethics.

The subject matter of business ethics reflects its mixed origins. In crude terms, it can be described as the union of business and society studies with mainstream business studies subjects through the medium of moral philosophy along with environmental issues relevant to business. What results is attention to the ethical aspects of any and all the many different areas of business activity (accounting, marketing, human resource management, and so on), with the activity also examined in terms of the ethical dimension to the economic, legal, political, and environmental context in which it is carried out at both a local and global level. The range of topics this can cover is vast and varied. Moreover, new areas of study are constantly **emerging** in the wake of developments such as globalisation, e-commerce, and accounting scandals such as Enron.

There is a great deal of congruence, with certain broad areas emerging as more or less standard. They divide, roughly speaking, into four very general and inevitably overlapping categories.

(a) First comes very reflexive and often very theoretical questions to do with the nature of business ethics as a subject and the application of ethical theory to business.

(b) Then come questions to do with the responsibilities and accountability of businesses and, in particular, large corporations.

(c) Then come what can be called *'functional'* questions to do with particular areas of activity (accounting, marketing, and so on).

(d) Finally we have what might be called *'global'* questions to do with the rights and wrongs of particular economic systems along with questions concerning international business and the natural environment.

 ACTIVITY 7  application

How ethical are you?

Visit www.ethicsandbusiness.org/cases.htm provided by the Centre for Ethics and Business at Loyola Marymount University. Here you will find a cartoon Simone de Beauvoir leading you through some ethical dilemmas

At www.ibe.org.uk you will find a number of questionnaires and inventories to help you take stock of your own and your organisation's view on ethical issues. There are also links to other sites and resources associated with ethical issues and dimensions.

Title of questionnaire/inventory	Source	Topic areas
ROT (Rice orientation test)	Chris Rice	Attitudes towards ethical issues
The Business ethics questionnaire	Simon Webley	Attitudes towards business ethics
Ethical practices questionnaire	Simon Webley	Identifying the seriousness and importance of certain ethical and unethical practices

4.1 Are ethics a big issue?

You may be wondering just how much evidence there is of ethics becoming an important aspect of business strategy and policy. How transparent will organisations need to be?

Look at just a few of the '*news stories*' highlighted on the ibe website for a few days in May 2009.

(a) **Financial Times – Mafia links to Sicilian wind farms**

Anti-Mafia magistrates in Sicily have opened a sweeping investigation into the wind power sector. Local officials, entrepreneurs and crime gangs are suspected of collusion in the construction of lucrative wind farms before their eventual sale to multinational companies. Italian and EU subsidies for the building of wind farms (at highest guaranteed rates, £160 per kwh), for the electricity they produce have turned southern Italy into a highly attractive market exploited by organised crime. http://www.ft.com/cms/s/0/b69fdf3a-38d1-11de-8cfe-00144feabdc0.html

(b) **The Independent – Fair tipping law '*won't cost waiters their jobs*'**

The restaurant trade warning that 45,000 jobs could be lost when ministers outlaw the use of tips to top up the earnings of staff paid less than the minimum wage has been rejected by an official government study. The review by the Department for Business, Enterprise and Regulatory Reform (DBERR) is likely to pave the way for the practice to be made illegal in November. The government crackdown was promised in July 2008 following The Independent's "*Fair Tips, Fair Pay*" campaign but no date for implementing it has been set. The campaign uncovered evidence that some waiting staff were being paid as little as £3 an hour, as restaurants used tips and service charges to bring their wages up to the national minimum of £5.73 per hour. http://www.independent.co.uk/news/uk/home-news/fair-tipping-law-wont-cost-waiters-their-jobs-1678997.html

(c) **Personnel Today.com – HR must be on watch for directors' fraud**

HR must be extra-vigilant against a rise in fraud by company directors during the recession, a lawyer has warned. Statistics published by the government's UK Insolvency Service at the weekend revealed that the number of directors banned for criminal malpractice jumped by almost one third (31%), to 1,852 directors who were charged in the 12 months to March. Disqualification proceedings launched against directors for crimes such as fraud or theft rose by

72%, while cases of misappropriation of assets grew by almost 20%.
http://www.personneltoday.com/articles/2009/05/05/50531/hr-must-be-on-watch-for-directors-fraud.html

(d) **Financial Times – Shell at risk of investor pay revolt**

Royal Dutch Shell is facing the risk of a shareholder rebellion over pay for the second successive year after two influential investor advisory groups raised concerns about discretionary pay awards made to board-level executives. RiskMetrics, which provides advice on voting to investors including members of the National Association of Pension Funds, has recommended a vote against Shell's remuneration report at its annual meeting on May 19. The Association of British Insurers' voting service has also issued an "*amber top*" alert on Shell's pay report, warning its members of a potential breach of good governance.

(e) **Financial Times – FSA threatens City with higher fines**

Financial wrongdoers could face significantly higher fines from the City watchdog under proposals it is due to put forward this summer. Hector Sants, chief executive of the Financial Services Authority, on Tuesday told City lawyers that the regulator was considering a "*new framework*" for the penalties it imposed, which would include higher fines. "The rationale for this is a perception that financial penalties have not been sufficiently large to deter wrongdoing in large institutions," he told the Financial Services Lawyers Association. The lawyers, many of whom follow the FSA's deliberations closely, expressed surprise at the announcement. http://www.ft.com/cms/s/0/d053ba60-39bb-11de-b82d-00144feabdc0.html

(f) **Financial Times – Investors turn militant over director pay**

The shareholder voting season across Europe is just getting into full swing but already the militancy of investors is noticeable in the wake of the financial crisis. Xstrata suffered a stinging protest by shareholders over its pay policies on Tuesday as more than a third of votes cast on its remuneration report at its annual meeting failed to back it. BP experienced a similar protest vote against its remuneration plan last month and pay is expected to be a contentious issue at Shell's annual meeting this month. http://www.ft.com/cms/s/0/d867b402-39a9-11de-b82d-00144feabdc0.html

(g) **BBC News – Speed camera boss in 100mph drive**

The boss of a speed camera firm has been banned from driving for six months after admitting speeding at more than 100mph on a 70mph road in Suffolk. Tom Riall, 49, is a chief executive of Serco, which has provided more than 5,000 speed cameras in the UK. He appeared at Sudbury Magistrates' Court and pleaded guilty to driving at 102.9mph on the A14 on 4 January, 2009. http://news.bbc.co.uk/1/hi/england/suffolk/8035511.stm

(h) **Financial Times – Shareholders to adopt tougher stance**

"No" votes at annual meetings will become more frequent as investors become tougher on companies, a leading figure in the asset management industry warned. Investors would no longer shy away from voting against board proposals, as they have in the past, said Michael McLintock, chief executive of M&G, which is owned by Prudential and is one of the UK's top three investment institutions. He was speaking at a conference of the Association of British Insurers and the CBI, aimed at looking at ways of restoring confidence in capital markets. http://www.ft.com/cms/s/0/4ea00fa2-3a7c-11de-8a2d-00144feabdc0.html

(i) **Financial Times – Windows release sparks complaints**

Microsoft has stirred up fresh complaints of anti-competitive behaviour with its release this week of a late-stage trial version of the next Windows PC operating system. The complaints, from some of the leading makers of web browsers, look set to intensify the software company's regulatory headaches just as it is seeking to head off swingeing anti-trust action from the European Commission over a related issue. The latest row has been stirred up by provisions in the next version of the operating system, known as Windows 7, which rivals say give an unfair advantage to Microsoft's own browser. http://www.ft.com/cms/s/0/4621afa2-3a6d-11de-8a2d-00144feabdc0.html

Take a look at the paper today or the latest news reports for further insights.

ACTIVITY 8   application

Marketing and Morality

Visit the CIM website and take time to consider one of the Shape the Agenda articles '*Marketing and Morality*'. You can see this is a topic of considerable importance in the practice of marketing, and ethical marketing practices cover everything from promotion to pricing strategy.

When you have read the article take a look at your own marketing activity – how far along the moral pathway have your business practices travelled?

Draw up a list of recommendations you would make for a Code of Conduct for marketers working in your sector.

4.2 Fairtrade

 MARKETING AT WORK   application

One example of ethics at work in the marketing arena is the growth of Fair Trade products.

Visit www.fairtrade.org.uk/ for more examples, cases and insights into the changes in this context. You can see consumer interest is growing.

4.2.1 Sales of Fairtrade certified products in the UK

Estimated UK retail sales by value 1999-2009 (£ million)

	1999	2000	2001	2002	2003	2004	2005	2006	2007	2008	2009
Coffee	15.0	15.5	18.6	23.1	34.3	49.3	65.8	93.0	117.0	137.3	157.0
Tea	4.5	5.1	5.9	7.2	9.5	12.9	16.6	25.1	30.0	64.8	68.1
Chocolate/cocoa	2.3	3.6	6.0	7.0	10.9	16.5	21.9	29.7	25.5	26.8	44.2
Honey products	n/a	0.9	3.2	4.9	6.1	3.4	3.5	3.4	2.7	5.2	4.6
Bananas	n/a	7.8	14.6	17.3	24.3	30.6	47.7	65.6	150.0	184.6	209.2
Flowers	n/a	n/a	n/a	n/a	n/a	4.3	5.7	14.0	24.0	33.4	30.0
Wine	n/a	n/a	n/a	n/a	1.5	3.3	5.3	8.2	10.0	16.4	
Cotton	n/a	n/a	n/a	n/a	n/a	0.2	4.5	34.8	77.9	50.1	
Other	n/a	n/a	2.2	3.5	7.2	22.3	30.3	45.7	100.8	172.6	219.4
TOTAL	21.8	32.9	50.5	63.0	92.3	140.8	195.0	286.3	493.0	712.6	799.0

(Source: Fair Trade Association, 2010)

"The global economic downturn made 2009 an incredibly tough year for the world's poor seeking a fair deal for their produce, the Fairtrade Foundation will tell stakeholders at a evening reception today in London to mark the launch of Fairtrade Fortnight 2010 (22 February – 7 March 2010). The global economic turndown has been felt worst in developing countries, where an estimated 50-90 million more people were thrown into extreme poverty in 2009, according to UN Millennium Development Goal figures. Meanwhile, here in the UK, just over 7 in 10 people told YouGov that they cut back on their personal budgets in some way as a result of the recession, such as eating out less. Yet the UK public has remained staunchly loyal, resulting in another increase in the value of Fairtrade sales, up on 2008 by 12% to an estimated retail value of over £799m, and 71% (who don't already buy everything they can Fairtrade) of people say they are willing to swap one or more products to Fairtrade in the next two weeks, according to the new YouGov poll commissioned by the Foundation."

www.fairtrade.org.uk/press_office/press_releases_and_statements/february_2010 - accessed 7th June 2010

When it comes to brand awareness the TNS CAPI Omnibus findings (2008) showed that 70% of the population recognise the FAIRTRADE Mark. Findings also show understanding of the concept behind the Mark has increased, with 64% of the population linking the Mark to a better deal for producers in the developing world (Fair Trade Association, 2009).

Marketers need to ask themselves how soon will Fairtrade be expected rather than an opportunity for differentiation.

4.3 New ways of engaging with customers

CSR and ethics are about how you do business. Other emerging themes at this level involve the ways in which we can engage customers and in particular the use of mobile and new media from developing SMS campaigns to networking sites like Face Book and Myspace or LinkedIn for business contacts.

Today marketers can use You Tube to promote their products. By May 2009 the original Cadbury's Eyebrows clip had been viewed by 3,588,020 people (not necessarily unique views) but a clear illustration of '*permission marketing*'.

New special interest sites mean that customers are clearly choosing what they want to know about and the style of communication they prefer.

And does this new media give customers more power?

It certainly provides a forum for marketers to find out what customers really want and help co-create products and services. One way communication is giving way to dialogue and that may be challenging for how we do things in the future.

Learning objective review

Learning objectives	Covered
1 Describe how marketing's role in business is changing and 'scope' this new world for marketing	☑ From a seller's market with limited role for marketing to a buyer's market where competitive advantage is key to winning and retaining customers and evolving to take account of the broader stakeholder agenda. ☑ You assessed the current role of marketing in your organisation.
2 Recommend ways in which marketers need to build new skills and approaches to fulfilling this changing role.	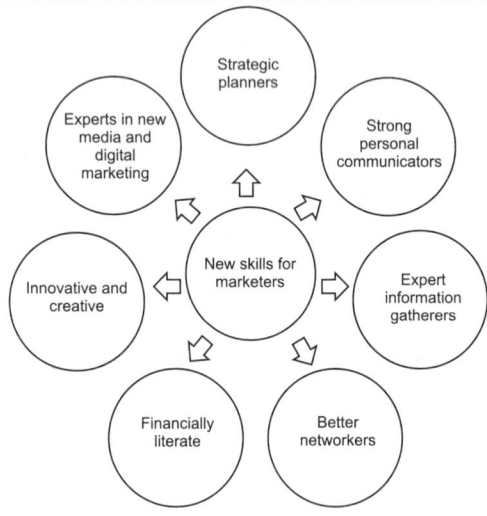 ☑ We examined the range of new skills marketers need in order to meet the demands from a new more strategic role. Today marketers need to be more analytical and professional planners
3 Discuss some of the '*new*' strategies being followed by business and consider the implications of these.	☑ We identified some of the current business strategies being adopted in different sectors. 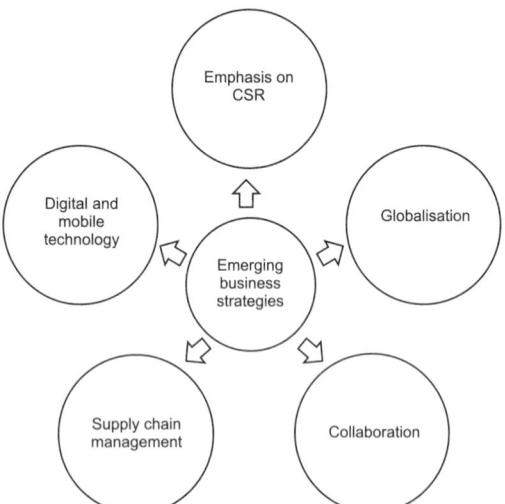 ☑ We examined both the question of ethics in business and its impact on marketing and how digital marketing is changing how we engage customers. We also focused specifically on CSR – considered the importance of the Triple Bottom Line and the broadening stakeholder agenda. ☑ We used the Value Chain to assess how CSR could be embedded across the business. ☑ We looked at one aspect of CSR – sustainability.

Emerging Themes

4 Assess a specific emerging theme, assess its impacting on a specific organisation and use scenario planning to help 'vision' different futures and consider the implications on a specific organisation	☑ We considered how one aspect of sustainability could be viewed as an emerging theme – water shortage.
	☑ We used scenario plans to consider the possible impact of future water shortages.
	☑ We continued to consider how these scenarios might impact on your organisation.

Quick quiz

1. How has the role of marketing evolved/ is continuing to change?
2. What advice does Gary Hamel give us about preparing for the future?
3. Why are scenario plans useful in this process?
4. Give two examples of developments that are leading to emerging issues in the area of business ethics.
5. What is assessed in the triple bottom line?

Activity debriefs

1 **How do you see our role emerging?**

Marketers' role will be:

(1) To ensure there is an external focus and awareness of what is happening in the market place, providing customer insight and a commentary on emerging themes.

(2) To ensure that marketing is 'positioned' effectively internally. No matter how good the external focus is, it can only impact on business performance if it is listened to, and acted upon. This means a much more strategic role for marketing with a broad appreciation of its role as 'architects of competitive advantage.'

(3) Innovation and creativity are needed to help create offers that deliver competitive advantage – marketers need to be a source of innovation and also have the skills needed to bring together the 'ingredients' of the offer to ensure integration and consistent positioning.

(4) In future communication with customers is more likely to be a dialogue than a broadcast – how we use new media, social networks and manage permission marketing will be on our agenda for some years to come.

2 **Who else may be involved?**

The answer to this question will vary across organisations and sectors but your answers could have included:

(a) HR teams responsible for employee relations and the employee brand.

(b) Corporate PR teams who may be responsible for broader community communications and media relations. This role may not be managed by marketing but report directly to the MD or chairman.

(c) Finance teams can take the lead with shareholder and financial media.

(d) Some organisations employ a CSR manger or director.

(e) Smaller companies may find that the owners or senior management teams take direct responsibility for these broader stakeholder issues.

5: Emerging themes within organisations

3   **Assessing the current role of marketing in your organisation.**

    No two organisations are the same when it comes to how they view, use and organise the marketing function. Some, for example the public sector, are still relatively new converts to the value of marketing. Others like FMCG firms have a long history of marketing activity.

4   This activity will depend on your own research.

5   Your list will be sector specific but you might have included some or all of the following:

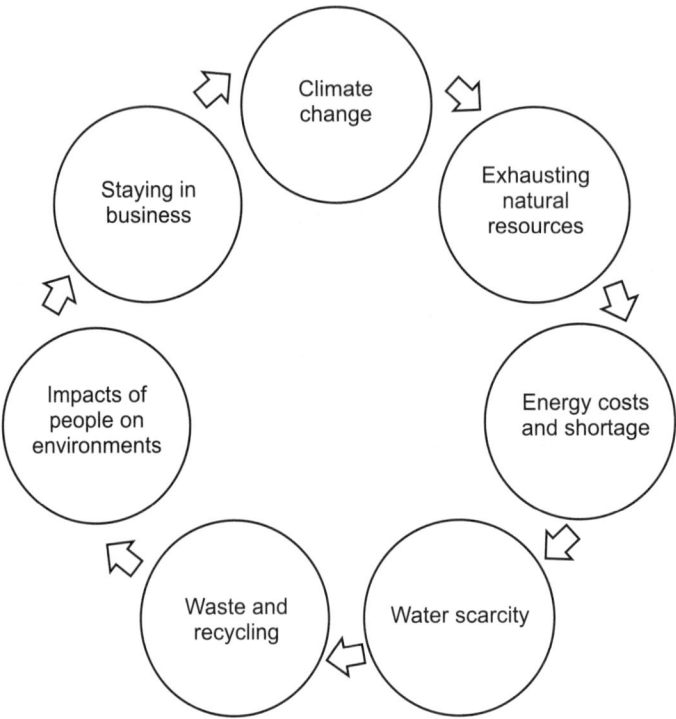

6   General Electric aims to cut its own use of water by 20% and is planning for heavy investment in recycling technologies.

    Recognising that the next problem to afflict the global economy (after soaring oil and food prices) will be a surge in the cost of water brought on by growing scarcity, General Electric is taking steps now.

    GE have said they will cut their own use of water by 20% by 2012 and export water-saving and recycling technology to countries (often emerging economies) hit by shortages. Jeff Immelt, Chief Executive, said in Beijing: 'We believe that, just as greenhouse gas emissions have been a big societal challenge, the same is true of water.'

    The move by GE comes as scientists are warning that 50% of the world's nations will be hit by water shortages by 2025 and 75% by 2050. Barcelona is already importing water from France.

    You can read the whole article at the Guardian website.

    Source: David Gow – The Guardian, Thursday 29 May 2008

7–8 These activities will depend on your own research

Quiz answers

1   As the orientation and strategy of business has evolved so has the role of marketing within the business.

    (a)   More strategic

    (b)   More holistic

    (c)   The key value driver for the business

    (d)   More analytical

    (e)   More financially literate

2   Hamel's advice:

    (a)   Have foresight to vision the future

    (b)   Consider what you would need to do to compete in that future

    (c)   Build the capabilities and competencies you need to prepare for that future.

3   Scenario plans allow you to consider a number of different 'futures' and consider the implications of these at sector or organisational level.

4   Emerging aspects of ethics in business are the result of developments such as globalisation, e-commerce, and accounting scandals such as Enron.

5   The triple bottom line assesses economic, social and environmental performance or organisations.

References

Davies, J (2009) *"Experts warn of major water shortage"* Farmers Guardian, 31st March 2009 available online at: http://www.farmersguardian.com/experts-warn-of-major-uk-water-shortage/24284.article [accessed 21st June 2009].

Fair Trade Association (2010) Facts and Figures, available online at: http://www.fairtrade.org.uk/what_is_fairtrade/facts_and_figures.aspx, [accessed 7th June 2010].

Hatton, A. (2000) The Definitive Guide to Marketing Planning, Prentice Hall, Harlow.

Vidal, J.(2006) *"Cost of water shortage: civil unrest, mass migration and economic collapse"* The Guardian, 17th August 2006, London.

Key concept

A bend in a trend, 26

Change drivers, 38
Competition for attention, 12

Devolution, 56

Emerging themes, 10

Fad, 26
Futurology, 30

Network governance, 63

Relevance, 12

Trend, 26

Index

Aging population, 41
Ansoff matrix, 7
Assessing sources, 46

Business markets, 67
Business Reality, 9
Buyer's market, 11

Change, 6
Changing attitudes, 55
Changing role, 82
Climate, 58
Climate change, 72
Collaboration, 65
Collaborative supplier relationships, 65
Collecting environmental information, 26
Consumer markets, 66
Contemporary issues, 10
Corporate Social Responsibility, 12, 13
Cultural change, 68
Customer behaviour, 63
Customisation, 64

De-centralisation, 58
Dell Computers, 64
Delphi Oracle, 29
Demographic changes, 66
Devolution, 56
Drivers of change, 38
Drivers of obesity, 39

E Reader, 70
Environment, 71
E-relationships, 64
Expert forecasts, 28

Force field analysis, 40
Forecast, 43
Forecasting, 25
Futurology, 30

Hamel, 4, 5, 16
Helicopter Vision, 22

Identifying key drivers, 24
Identifying trends, 25
Impact on marketing practice, 46
Industry level sensing, 27
Innovation, 47

Internal customer relationships, 64

Joint ventures, 64
Jury forecasts, 28

Law, 59
Legal environment, 58

Macro environmental forces, 24
Market Maps, 23
Market scanning, 20
Market sensing, 27
Marketers' role, 81
Marketing myopia, 20
Migration, 66
Mission statements, 21

Nanotechnology, 70
Network governance, 63
Networks, 64
Newspaper sector, 70

Opportunities, 7
Opportunity/threat Matrix, 31

Packaging decisions, 72
Partnerships, 64
PEST, 3, 16, 18
Planning gap, 6
Political attitudes, 58
Political climate, 56
Pollution, 72
Porter's Five Forces, 22, 44
Pralahad, 5

Recession, 61

Scenario planning, 29, 32
Seller's market, 10
Single person households, 68
Social, 68
Sources of information, 45
Stakeholder agenda, 12
STEEPLE, 3, 16, 18
Strategic alliances, 64
Strategic wear-out, 4
Strategies for business, 85
Supplier partnerships, 65

Systems, 58

Technology, 71
Trend analysis, 25, 28
Triple bottom line, 12

Virtual organisations, 64

Waste, 72
Water shortage, 88

Notes

Review form & Free prize draw

All original review forms from the entire BPP range, completed with genuine comments, will be entered into one of two draws on 31 January 2011 and 31 July 2011. The names on the first four forms picked out on each occasion will be sent a cheque for £50.

Name: _____ Address: _____

_____

_____

1. How have you used this Text?
(Tick one box only)

☐ Self study (book only)
☐ On a course: college_____
☐ Other _____

3. Why did you decide to purchase this Text?
(Tick one box only)

☐ Have used companion Assessment workbook
☐ Have used BPP Texts in the past
☐ Recommendation by friend/colleague
☐ Recommendation by a lecturer at college
☐ Saw advertising in journals
☐ Saw website
☐ Other _____

2. During the past six months do you recall seeing/receiving any of the following?
(Tick as many boxes as are relevant)

☐ Our advertisement in *The Marketer*
☐ Our brochure with a letter through the post
☐ Saw website

4. Which (if any) aspects of our advertising do you find useful?
(Tick as many boxes as are relevant)

☐ Prices and publication dates of new editions
☐ Information on product content
☐ Facility to order books off-the-page
☐ None of the above

5. Have you used the companion Assessment Workbook? Yes ☐ No ☐

6. Have you used the companion Passcards? Yes ☐ No ☐

7. Your ratings, comments and suggestions would be appreciated on the following areas.

	Very useful	Useful	Not useful
Introductory section (How to use this text, study checklist, etc)	☐	☐	☐
Introduction	☐	☐	☐
Syllabus linked learning outcomes	☐	☐	☐
Activities and Marketing at Work examples	☐	☐	☐
Learning reviews	☐	☐	☐
Magic Formula references	☐	☐	☐
Index	☐	☐	☐
Structure and presentation	☐	☐	☐

	Excellent	Good	Adequate	Poor
Overall opinion of this Text	☐	☐	☐	☐

8. Do you intend to continue using BPP CIM Range Products? ☐ Yes ☐ No

9. Have you visited bpp.com/lm/cim? ☐ Yes ☐ No

10. If you have visited bpp.com/lm/cim, please give a score out of 10 for its overall usefulness /10

Please note any further comments and suggestions/errors on the reverse of this page.

Please return to: Rebecca Hart, BPP Learning Media, FREEPOST, London, W12 8BR.

If you have any additional questions, feel free to email cimrange@bpp.com

Emerging Themes

Review form & Free prize draw (continued)

Please note any further comments and suggestions/errors below.

Free prize draw rules

1. Closing date for 31 January 2011 draw is 31 December 2010. Closing date for 31 July 2011 draw is 30 June 2011.

2. Restricted to entries with UK and Eire addresses only. BPP employees, their families and business associates are excluded.

3. No purchase necessary. Entry forms are available upon request from BPP Learning Media. No more than one entry per title, per person. Draw restricted to persons aged 16 and over.

4. Winners will be notified by post and receive their cheques not later than 6 weeks after the relevant draw date. List of winners will be supplied on request.

5. The decision of the promoter in all matters is final and binding. No correspondence will be entered into.

Emerging Themes